Table of Contents

I.	How to Use This Program	3
	Classical Historian Teacher Certification Requirements	4
II.	What is Classical Education in History?	5
III.	The Thinking Tools of the Historian	7
IV.	Six Essential Thinking Tools of the Historian	13
	1. Fact or Opinion?	13
	2. Judgment	15
	3. Supporting Evidence	16
	4. Primary or Secondary Source Analysis	17
	5. Using Quotes	18
	6. Paraphrasing	19
V.	Open-Ended History Questions	20
	A. Types of Questions	20
	B. The Influences of History	21
VI.	The Fall of the Roman Empire,	22
	7. The Fall of the Roman Empire	23
VII.	Teaching with the Socratic Discussion,	26
	8. Teaching with the Socratic Discussion	26
	9. Socratic Discussion Fall of the Roman Empire	29
VIII.	The Writing Process for a One-Paragraph Assignment	30
	10. Thesis Statement	31
	11. Outline for a One-Paragraph Essay	32
	12. Rough Draft for a One-Paragraph Essay	34
	13. Revising	36
IX.	Advanced Thinking Tools of the Historian	37
	14. Counterargument	37
	15. Analyzing Primary Sources	38
	16. Cause and Effect	39
	17. Compare and Contrast	40

X.	The Writing Process for a Five-Paragraph Assignment	41
	A. Thesis for a Five-Paragraph Essay	41
	B. Outline for a Five-Paragraph Essay	43
	C. Rough Draft for a Five-Paragraph Essay	46
XI.	Grading Essays	49
	A. One-Paragraph Essay Grading Rubric	51
	B. Five-Paragraph Essay Grading Rubric	53
	C. Student Sample Essays and Grades	54
XII.	The Essential Tools of Literary Analysis	72
XIII.	Encouraging Family Discussion at the Dinner Table	76

I. How To Use This Program

This program provides the teacher with the philosophical understanding to teach classical education in history and with concrete lessons that can be used immediately.

This book is not a stand-alone text, but needs to be used in conjunction with *The Teaching the Socratic Discussion in History DVD program*, or in conjunction with the live training offered by The Classical Historian, or, in conjunction with the Digital Videos located in The Dolphin Society.

The DVD program and the live training were created out of demand from teachers who wanted a step-by-step explanation of how to teach their students the Socratic discussion in history. The teacher is advised to watch the DVDs and follow along in this book *before* teaching to students using the Classical Historian materials.

Classical Historian Teacher Certification Requirements

For a Basic Certification:

1. Complete all activities in this book and watch The Tools of the Historian DVDs as shown in The Dolphin Society in digital format or on the DVDs.

2. Obtain the Ancient and Medieval Civilizations DVD.

3. Watch the Socratic Discussions on Ancient Civilizations and complete the following activities:
> Choose one Socratic Discussion that you think exhibits best student use of critical thinking skills. Explain in a one-paragraph essay how you think this discussion shows student usage of critical thinking skills. Explain how the teacher drew out the critical thinking skills of the students.

4. Watch the Socratic Discussions on Medieval Civilizations and complete the following activities:
> Choose one Socratic Discussion that you think exhibits best student use of critical thinking skills. Explain in a one-paragraph essay how you think this discussion shows student usage of critical thinking skills. Explain how the teacher drew out the critical thinking skills of the students.

For an Advanced Certification:

4. Over the course of the year, collect two one-paragraph and two five-paragraph essays that you've graded, according to the rubrics in this book. Write a short paragraph explaining your grading.

Mail in or email (john@classicalhistorian.com) all work that you've done to the following address: The Classical Historian, 1019 Domador, San Clemente, CA 92673. Within one month, you will receive a written response of all of your work and written notification if you have attained the Advanced Teacher certification from the Classical Historian. Your teaching information will be posted on our website. You may turn in this coursework at any time.

II. What is Classical Education in History?

Classical education in the humanities refers to an educational approach that is used to teach the subjects of the humanities. The humanities are academic subjects that study the human condition, using methods that are primarily analytical, critical, or speculative. Dorothy Sayers was an English writer who spearheaded the beginning of the classical approach to education in modern times. Writing in twentieth-century Great Britain, she wrote in "The Lost Tools of Learning" that students need first to learn the analytical tools of learning before they learn a variety of "subjects." She separated a student's life into three stages: 1. Grammar 2. Dialectic 3. Rhetoric

The Grammar stage is appropriate to the child before the age of 11 or 12. Sayers called this stage the "Poll Parrot" because the child is so intent at pleasing his parent that he will parrot whatever the parent teaches him. I've met many parents of children at age ten who are so worried their children are not independent thinkers, and they worry that there is something wrong with their teaching. Don't Worry! Rejoice! It is a beautiful thing to work with a child before he becomes argumentative. In the Grammar Stage, it is enough if the child spends time reading interesting stories of history, memorizing simple historical facts, and has an idea where continents and countries are located.

Near the age of 12 or so, when a child begins to express his own thoughts and seems to want to argue intellectually, he has then entered this second stage, what Sayers called the Dialectic. In this stage, the student is ready and capable of learning the tools of learning. In the study of history, these tools include but are not limited to the following: distinguishing fact from opinion, developing good judgment from historical evidence, critiquing various historical sources, understanding the various influences on history, the Socratic discussion, and writing analytical essays. It is with the student in the dialectic stage that I have spent the majority of my teaching career.

For the past 14 years, I have taught 6th, 7th and 8th graders Language Arts and Social Studies. I have to confess, that I never wanted to teach this grade level because it seemed like punishment to work with this age. However, I have found that I love this age. The student is analytically capable of understanding nearly every argument that exists. The student is incredibly open-minded, and will not label his teacher a liberal or conservative after the first day. This student is also like a sponge, able to soak up incredible amounts of knowledge. And finally, at this age, the student still likes or even loves the teacher, even if he or she won't say it. For those who home school, this is a fascinating age.

In the final stage, Rhetoric, the student continues to use the tools of learning and works on perfecting his ability to speak and write. The student in the Rhetoric stage should be given more primary sources to read and analyze and spend less time working with a textbook. The student should be introduced to the great thinkers and writings of all time.

It is unfortunate, but in the public school system, a teacher very often has to keep the focus of class entirely on the grammar stage. Nervous to finish the curriculum and cover all the standards, he has to sacrifice teaching thinking methods to drilling students with basic facts. This student may leave school unprepared for the world. As Sayers wrote of students, "They are a prey to words in their emotions instead of being the masters of them in their intellects. We, who were scandalized in 1940 when men were sent to fight armored tanks with rifles, are not scandalized when young men and women are sent into the world to fight massed propaganda with a smattering of "subjects". Our children will never learn to analyze history with such a curriculum, and will remain in the Grammar Stage of intellectual development.

The study of history is a perfect subject to practice the skills of the Dialectic and Rhetoric Stage. History is such an excellent subject to practice analysis and logic because it is something that is more concrete than philosophy. It is a concrete subject, meaning there are real people and events to practice the skills of logic and rhetoric. Presented in a discussion format, history is interesting, because it involves the analysis of the student. As many historical events can be viewed from a variety of perspectives, history is a topic that is conducive to discussion. Did the North have to go to war against the South in the American Civil War? What was the main cause of the fall of the Roman Empire? Was Napoleon a hero or a villain? Was America's westward expansion in the 1800s a triumph or a tragedy? Discussing and debating these topics hone the student's skills of Logic and Rhetoric.

Students taught in the skills of the Dialectic and Rhetoric in history are also able to analyze our modern media. How many times have we seen a "shocking headline" on an internet news service's home page, only to learn a day later that it was untrue? How many times have you read about the same event presented in two very contrasting perspectives from two different wire services? One goal in history education is to teach students the value of analyzing news sources and recognizing bias. When students can determine the political perspectives of the major news gathering services in the United States, they will be more able to question the claims of journalists and politicians. We want our children to be citizens ready to not only be well-informed, but to also be able to decipher the truth from the media.

III. The Thinking Tools of the Historian

The tools of the secondary school historian were not created by me. I have only placed them in a format that is easily accessible for young students, and simple to use for very busy teachers. Credit is due to Jacques Barzun and Henry F. Graff for authoring *The Modern Researcher*, published by Harcourt Braced Jovanovich College Publishers in 1992, and Carl Gustavson for authoring *A Preface to History*, published by McGraw-Hill Book Company, Inc. in 1955. These two books provided me with understanding of skills necessary to analyze history. They also inspired me to create something that my students could use. Credit is also due to Professor Howard Hunt of Cal State Dominguez Hills, who assigned me these books and mentored me in my graduate studies. Lastly, and maybe most importantly, 20 years in the classroom as a teacher, and over 16 years in the classroom as a student, has made it apparent to me that the student wants to learn, be inspired, be challenged, and attempt to go beyond himself to strive for perfection in the academic world. To do this, the lessons have to be presented in an understandable format, accessible and logical. Lessons also have to give freedom to the student to create, to imagine, and to express. Following is an explanation of various tools of the historian.

Lessons for these tools can be found in each of the Take a Stand! books. It is strongly recommended that over one year of instruction, each student learns and practices these tools of the historian. **Before lesson one, students and teachers should complete the Essential Tools of the Historian, as found on DVD #2.**

Tool #1
Distinguishing Fact from Opinion

One essential task of the historian is to distinguish between opinion and fact. In the classroom, I found out very fast how my students could not do this without training and practice. What I had thought they already knew, I found that most students under eighteen have had no instruction on the difference between opinion and fact. Often times, people will think that if it is said on television, then it is true.

Unfortunately, these students may have only learned history from teachers who tell them what they think happened and why. As educated adults, we know this idea of history is completely false. Consider the varying opinions on the Iraq War during the years of the 43rd President, George H. W. Bush. If you were to ask well-educated adults their opinions about this war, the reasons it started, its success or failure, and its effect on the United States, you will get very different answers, because very few people bother to read in various sources and to find the truth in history.

Tool #2
Forming Good Judgment

For students, historical judgment is one of the key elements of education that is lacking. However, it is normal in other subjects for the teacher to require students to use judgment. It is very common in the Language Arts classroom to ask students to tell what they think about a particular character in a novel, or to try to persuade somebody to think that the school dress code is onerous. In Science, good teachers encourage students to perform experiments to test their hypotheses, then to examine the results and form opinions from these results. In classes that used to be available, for example Music Appreciation and Art, students were allowed to say their own opinion regarding these artistic creations. How has history become the dead beat when it comes to analysis and critical thinking? It is in history where opinion, analysis, and judgment are essential to a quality education. If our students leave the school system unable to make decisions based on the evidence, how do we think they will be able to choose the best job, the best home mortgage, or the best car loan? Giving our students facts to memorize and telling them how to think prepares them to be robots, not responsible citizens. Do we want the future generation to be equipped with facts but unable to figure out their meaning? Without proper training and practice in judgment, our youth are susceptible to those who want to manipulate them into thinking a certain way or buying particular products they do not need.

Forming judgment and defending one's ideas are the most exciting elements of the history class. Once students realize that their opinions differ from their classmates, and that they don't have to mimic the teacher's ideas, history becomes a living subject, a study whose meaning is determined in part by students. Instead of the student just trying to give the teacher what he thinks the teacher wants, the student becomes an active academic, deciding what the relevance of history is. Below is an introductory lesson that can be used with students learning judgment. Although it may appear to be very simple, it is effective in communicating the idea that each individual can form good judgment when given enough facts.

Tool #3
Supporting Evidence

Supporting evidence refers to everything you use to support your main idea. It does not include peripheral information that may be interesting, but is not necessary to get your point across. Understanding and using supporting evidence properly is necessary in forming and making good judgment. If our students cannot distinguish good supporting evidence from poor supporting evidence, our society will be one where people will believe whatever they are told to believe based on nothing more than an opinion. How many times have we heard from a so-called expert an opinion that is not backed up by evidence? Turn on any news station and try to determine if the broadcaster uses more opinion than fact in making judgment. Do certain stations seem to promote more opinion-based analysis and others more fact-based analysis? Unfortunately, many of our students are not learning these simple lessons. To some, sources of information are more important than the information itself. In some circumstances, how something is said or written is more important than what is said or written.

One problem with supporting evidence is what it is not. Many young students, when faced with an essay assignment in history, will throw the facts on paper thinking that, if their paper is full of facts then the teacher will reward them. Unfortunately for the student, this should be further from the truth. In one assignment from my classroom of eighth graders, I ask students to decide if George Washington was necessary for the success of the American Revolution. Without failure, there are a few students who attempt to place as many facts as possible in their answer. These facts, however, have nothing to do with Washington being responsible. They are about the dates he was born and died, his wife's biographical information, or where he lived and farmed.

Proper training in the use of supporting evidence is necessary to train young students to be analytical thinkers and decision-makers. In the lesson below, students are introduced to the idea of supporting evidence then complete a practice exercise to begin familiarizing themselves to this idea.

Tool #4
Making the Textbook Accessible

Because of circumstances beyond my control, history textbooks tend to be dry and without excitement or controversy. Due to this fact, students find reading informational materials in history very boring. Whatever is boring is hard to remember, as what does not catch the human spirit tends to be quickly forgotten. Perhaps that is one reason that some people say, "I don't remember anything I learned in history."

Reading with a purpose is the answer that solves the problem of getting students to read the textbook. Once students know that they have to make a choice in the interpretive question, their reading becomes their personal research. Focused on finding information that makes their argument stronger or on evidence that disputes their perspective allows students to navigate through the information they do not need to read. Reading with a purpose helps students focus on the essential, and gives them an internal motivation for reading.

Along with an interpretive question that focuses reading, younger students need reading aids that help them along the way. A graphic organizer to fill in, or questions to answer that are specific to the research goal, will help students not take too many notes. The following is an example from an assignment where students are asked to research contributions of ancient civilizations and determine which contributions were most important to humanity. Providing students with a framework in which to tackle reading informational reading is an excellent way to foster good readers.

Tool #5
Analyzing Primary Sources

The use of primary sources is essential to the most advanced study of history. It is here where the student comes into direct contact with the source itself, without any intermediary analysis by experts and teachers. However, because of limits of language ability and practice, primary sources may be too challenging for a lower level English Learner or younger student. It is for these reasons that I recommend, at least in the beginning of study, only using a good textbook. If you don't have one in your school, then please find supplements! I know it is very challenging to find good secondary source materials without so many pictures and misplaced items. However, our students have to start somewhere, and a good teacher can also provide quality summaries of history his students can use. As soon as the student is ready, introduce primary sources. The more primary sources the student has to analyze the better, and usually, the better-rounded the argument and paper, in terms of learning all of the varying perspectives.

Tool #6
Using Quotes

When making an argument, it is often important to show that your idea is supported by others who are working in the field. On television news, "experts" frequently give their opinion on a wide range of topics. It is thought that since they are experts, they should know. Sometimes this is true, but even when it is not; it is sometimes advantageous to hear what others think.

More importantly than using modern-day experts, the writer is strongly encouraged to use quotes from historical figures. Quoting from Plato's Republic to illustrate what ancient man thought of philosophy and politics is very powerful. Quoting from autobiographies of historical figures who lived through great events lets the reader get a glimpse into the magic of primary sources. The excellent writer of essays will quote from period historical figures.

Tool #7
Paraphrasing

The adult may well remember that as a child, he stayed up late at night the evening before the fifth-grade project was due, taking sentences from an encyclopedia and changing the word order around so the teacher would not accuse him of copying. I remember this. I think the project was on the state of Nevada. While we were supposed to be reading and thinking about the information, often times this practice became an exercise of language, testing our ability to work with words.

It seems the student today has no practice in doing this. Younger students at times don't know the difference between copying and paraphrasing. For a homework assignment, I have my students research a person, or an event. Invariably, a few students come back the next day with printed sheets of copy from the internet. "Here are my notes, Mr. De Gree." Even though I explain to them beforehand that this is not acceptable, there are always a few who try to get by without thinking.

The skill of paraphrasing is an important one and one that can be easily learned and practiced in the history classroom. When researching a topic to find supporting evidence for a thesis, paraphrasing is crucial, and natural. It is crucial, because a thesis is only as good as the evidence that supports it. And it is natural, because when you are researching a topic to support a thesis, you will focus only on that information which is necessary for your paper, leaving out unnecessary items. The history paper is an excellent one to practice the skill of paraphrasing.

Tool # 8
Counterargument

The counterargument in a history paper is a must if you need the paper to be of the highest quality. The writer first presents the supporting evidence for his thesis, making the strongest argument possible. Then, the author states the strongest argument against his own thesis and explains the rationale for this. After the essayists writes this counterargument, he then shows how it really is not as strong as some would have you believe. The writer, in effect, is taking the biggest argument of his opponent and showing that it is not that effective. It is as if the other side is having the wind taken from its sails.

This technique is an excellent skill to have, as it challenges the mind of the author to see things from various perspectives. Because the meaning of history is up to debate, it is essential that the historian be open-minded enough to entertain opposing viewpoints. The counterargument and refutation makes the paper stronger by showing that the thesis is stronger than the strongest argument from the opposing side.

Tool # 9
Cause and Effect

Cause and effect is an important aspect of historical reasoning. Unfortunately, as Carl Gustavson writes in *A Preface to History*, it is all too easy and common to turn to one person, or one party, as the cause of something. He gives as the example the tendency of young historians to attribute one cause to the Reformation. "It was Luther," or, "The Church was corrupt." These one-cause answers all answers are typical of a mind of a person who wished not to delve deeply and broadly into the variety of causes that may bring about events.

As I am writing this, the United States of America is in the middle of another hotly contested presidential election. The claims of the candidates are similar to those claims of the past elections.

"It's his fault."

"He's the reason everything is broken in Washington. If it wasn't for him, we would be in this mess."

"If you elect him, you'll make the terrorists happy. Our country won't be any safer, but in fact it will be more dangerous."

"If you elect him, America will be a place with more poor on the street."

These claims all adhere to the simplistic idea that one person can be the cause of huge events or massive movements in a country. While it is tempting to become emotionally involved in political debates, the historian has to try with effort to remain detached, and remember that it is a multitude of causes that bring about huge events. Making the claim that "Hitler started World War II" completely forgets Japan and the Soviet Union's appetite for territory, the Versailles Treaty, the demilitarization of France, the appeasement of Hitler by Chamberlain, and the thousand or so years of anti-Jewish ferment in Europe.

Of course, it may be challenging to teach the multiple levels of causation to young students, and so our task as teachers may be to just teach them that events have causes. Once we get past this point, we can teach them that typically, events have various causes, some more important than others. The student's job is to assess the importance of the various causes and to ascertain which cause was the most important.

Tool # 9
Cause and Effect

Cause and effect is a term that means one event made another event happen. For example, if you push against the pedals of your bicycle, the bicycle moves. In this example, the push against the pedals is the cause and the bicycle moving is the effect.

CAUSE	→EFFECT
push against pedals	→bicycle moves

In social studies, cause and effect usually relates events and people. The relationship is trickier to understand than the above example with the bicycle. Sometimes it is difficult to see causes and effects in history. Here are two examples from American history with which most historians would agree.

CAUSE	→EFFECT
Japan attacks Pearl Harbor	→the United States enters World War II
the U.S. drops atomic bombs on Japan	→Japan surrenders

Tool # 10
Compare and Contrast

While compare and contrast is not typically seen as an element of historical reasoning, it is commonly seen on tests in Language Arts and in Social Studies and is therefore an important skill for the student to learn. In addition to this necessity to understand the school system, when a student compares and contrasts different items, it allows him to see that people, movements, and countries often have similarities and differences. This very obvious notion for the adult teacher is often lost on the student.

The young, when analyzing history, often make the mistake of seeing and analyzing history only through the perspective of someone living in the current age. This perspective denies the idea that people change over time, that what is considered normal today wasn't considered normal in other times. In addition, this inability to leave oneself in order to understand other people is a type of complacent self-centeredness that an education should reveal and destroy. The skill of analyzing history involves understanding the mores of other times and other people. Only in doing so will it be possible to clearly see the events and people of the past.

IV. Six Essential Thinking Tools of the Historia
1. Fact or Opinion?

Fact

A **fact** in history is a statement that is accepted as true and is not debatable. A fact often refers to a date, a person, or a document. For example, "The Declaration of Independence was written and signed in 1776." We know this happened because we have the original document, the men who wrote and signed this document wrote about it, and observers wrote about it as well. There is no doubt in anybody's mind whether the facts in this statement are true.

Which of the following sentences are facts?

Fact or Not a Fact?

1. _____ In 1825 in the United States of America, every human was a citizen.

2. _____ The Romans were horrible architects.

3. _____ The Western Roman Empire was the best ancient empire in the world.

4. _____ The United States of America has 50 states.

5. _____ California has the best waves to surf in the United States.

Opinion

An **opinion** is an expression of somebody's ideas and is debatable. Opinions that are based on facts and good reasoning are stronger than opinions not based on facts. In history, opinions alone tend to be less persuasive than when a person supports his opinions with facts. Which of the following are opinions and which are facts?

Opinion or Fact?

1. _____ The Qur'an (Koran) is the holy book of the Muslims.

2. _____ Teachers who are nice don't assign homework.

3. _____ Almost everybody's favorite food is pizza.

4. _____ The North Pole is north of Europe.

5. _____ Independence day for the United States of America is July 4, 1776.

Now that you've learned the difference between fact and opinion, read the example paragraphs below and answer the questions. These two students attempted to answer the question "Did Roman civilization contribute anything that was good to the world?"

Student 1: Roman civilization contributed much to the world. First of all, Romans invented a lot of things. Romans invented Roman numerals. This helps the United States because when Americans have a Super Bowl; Roman numerals are used, like Super Bowl "XXXV." Secondly, early Romans were very tough people. Romans worked hard all day on their farms, and they didn't waste their time on needless parties like most Americans do. Furthermore, Romans were very clean people. All statues of Romans show them to be clean. One expert claimed that Romans took baths every day. Romans contributed to the world Roman numerals, a tough work ethic, and cleanliness.

Student 2: Roman civilization contributed much to the world. The language of the Romans, Latin, is the mother of many world languages. Spanish, French, Portuguese, and Romanian are all Latin languages, and English has many Latin roots. Secondly, Roman law is still used today in certain parts of the world. The Justinian Code, created by Emperor Justin, is still in use in France. The United States uses many elements of Roman law, such as the concept "innocent until proven guilty." And lastly, Romans kept alive great elements of Greek culture, such as Aesop's fables, which are read today in the United States. Roman civilization contributed to the world with Latin, Roman law, and literature.

Questions

1. Which of these two students uses more opinion than fact? _____

2. Copy one sentence that is an opinion. _____

3. Copy one sentence that details at least one fact. _____

4. Which of these two students' writings is more persuasive? Why? _____

2. Judgment

Judgment in social studies means a person's evaluation of facts. For example, if we use the fact that the Romans believed citizens could vote we can judge from this that the Romans looked somewhat favorably on democracy. Good judgment is very persuasive but bad judgment is not.

Answer the questions below based on the facts. Discuss your judgments in class.

Fact: 11-year-old Maria Perez won the gold medal in the one mile championship race for the United States.
Judgment: Is Maria a fast runner? _____
Fact: Private Smith was killed in war and had one wife and 7 children.
Judgment: Was Private Smith's death a tragedy?
Fact: Thursday's temperature in Santa Ana was 105 degrees Fahrenheit.
Judgment: Was Thursday a hot day?_____

Fact: Mark's baseball team beat all other teams by over 10 runs during the season.
Judgment:

Fact: The teacher assigned the 12 year olds three hours of homework every day during the school year.
Judgment:

Fact: Dad's new car broke down four times during the first month after he bought it.
Judgment:

3. Supporting Evidence

Supporting evidence refers to everything you use to support your thesis. These include, but are not limited to, the following.

1. Diaries and journals
2. Government documents such as birth certificates
3. Songs and stories
4. Coins, medals, jewelry
5. Artistic works such as pictures and paintings
6. Tools and pottery
7. Documents such as the Declaration of Independence
8. Weapons
9. Burial remains
10. Literature and customs

Good historians overwhelm the reader with so many pieces of supporting evidence that the writing will be quickly accepted. Also, the writer has a duty to explain carefully and logically the meaning of the evidence, showing how it supports the thesis. A writer must be careful, however, not to include unnecessary evidence. For example, the fact that Lincoln was born in a log cabin isn't evidence that he was a good president. Also, the dates a president was born and died may be evidence, but they would not support a thesis arguing who was the best president.

Practice Answer which of the following is evidence for the topic "Explain what daily life was like in the Roman Empire in the third century A.D."

1. A diary from 1984 _____
2. A newspaper article from A.D. 245 _____
3. Your friend likes the subject _____
4. A movie about life in the third century _____
5. A song Romans sang in 201 A.D. _____
6. The date Julius Caesar was born _____
7. A painting of a Roman slave working in 299 A.D. _____

4. Primary or Secondary Source Analysis

A **primary source** is a piece of evidence authored by a person who witnessed or experienced a historical event. For example, diaries and journals are primary sources. It is usually better to find out something from a person who experienced a particular event than to hear about it secondhand. Primary source documents are usually the most useful for historians.

A **secondary source** is a piece of evidence that has been worked on by somebody who was not a witness to the historical event. Examples of secondary sources are textbooks, documentaries, and encyclopedias. Secondary sources are valuable but not as valuable as primary sources. Secondary sources contain the bias of the writer. This means that the writer of a secondary source will put his ideas into his explanation of the historical event, even when he may be trying not to.

Take a look at these two examples regarding the same event

Event: A car accident outside of school

Example 1: "Oh no! I was in the back seat of my mom's car. This kid threw his friend's handball onto the street. All of a sudden, his friend jumped in front of my mom's car to get his ball. He didn't even look if a car was coming. My mom hit him and he was terribly injured. We called the paramedics right away and stayed there until he was taken away in an ambulance."

Example 2: "Did you hear what happened? Mario told me that his brother was walking home when he dropped his handball onto the street. After his brother looked both ways for cars, he stepped out onto the street to get his ball. Then this mad lady came speeding down the street and aimed her car at him. She hit him on purpose!"

Questions
1. Which is a primary source? _____
2. Which is a secondary source? _____
3. Which of these is more believable? Why? _____

5. Using Quotes

An effective analytical essay in social studies will use quotes. For example, an essay about the use of violence in the Middle Ages will be stronger if certain quotes from this time period are used. When you argue a point about the past, there is no better evidence than a primary source such as a quote.

Look at the example below. The paragraph is part of an answer to the question "Did seventh-century leaders use violence to rule?"

Some seventh-century leaders used the threat of violence to control their subjects. Ziyad Ibn Abihi, an emir (leader) of Mesopotamia, wrote in a public document A.D. 670, "Do not be carried away by your hatred and anger against me; it would go ill with you. I see many heads rolling; let each man see that his own head stays upon his shoulders." Obviously, this seventh-century leader used the threat of violence to control his people.

When using quotes, write the original author's name, and the speech or document from which the quote was taken. Introduce the quote, explaining its meaning in your own words. Then, write the quote. Punctuate correctly with quotation marks.

Practice

Practice introducing this quote from Socrates, an ancient Greek who lived in the 5th century B.C.

"Be slow to fall into friendship; but when thou art in, continue firm and constant."

Use correct punctuation! Pay attention to the commas, the quotation marks, and the end marks.

6. Paraphrasing

Paraphrasing means to take information from your research and to put it in your own words.

This is an important skill to have when writing a research paper. If you copy directly from a source such as a book, but do not place the words in quotation marks and write the author's name, it is called **plagiarism**. Plagiarism is against the rules of writing and your teacher should not accept the work!

Here is an example of paraphrasing a quote.

Quote:
The Tang Dynasty is often called a golden age in China because the Chinese created encyclopedias, poems, and silk, and because taxes were lowered.

Paraphrase:
One "golden age" in China happened during the Tang Dynasty. Chinese did great things and enjoyed freedoms. Taxes were lowered, and the Chinese created poems, encyclopedias, and silk.

Quote: "Confucius lived in a time of turmoil in China. He wrote about respecting parents and authority. Many Chinese grew to believe in what Confucius wrote about."
Paraphrase:
Quote: "The Chinese were great traders with other cultures. The Silk Road ran from China through central Asia to the Middle East. Along this trail, Chinese met with Arabs, Africans, Europeans, and other Asians.
Paraphrase:

V. Open-Ended History Questions

A. Types of Questions

The type of discussion you will lead depends in large part on the kind of question that is asked. If a teacher asks a question that has a clear yes or no answer, and only one option is available, there will obviously be no discussion. All of the questions used in the Take a Stand! books allow for multiple answers, and require the student to provide evidence to back up his assertion. In higher level high school and in college level history courses, there tends to be seven types of open-ended question types. These question types practice higher order thinking skills, as defined in Bloom's Taxonomy, because students must know the basics of the history, synthesize this information, independently make choices, and defend their answer with evidence and logic. However, even a 6th grader is able to use higher order thinking skills, and is in fact, ready and eager to do so.

In public and private high schools, the AP® classes (Advanced Placement) are considered the most advanced. A company, the College Board, is in charge of administering a test at the end of the year Students using college-level materials. Based on their score, students earn college credit. "Pre-AP®" refers to kids in grades 6-9 who are preparing for the more challenging assignments.

In undergraduate and graduate history courses, the same type of questions are found as in the more challenging high school classes. Below is a list of the seven types of questions used in these more rigorous courses. In the Take a Stand! books, each of the questions fits into one of the following question types.

1. Change Over Time
2. Cause and Effect
3. Compare and Contrast
4. Define and Identify
5. Statement/Reaction
6. Evaluation
7. Analyzing Viewpoints

B. The Influences of History

When studying history, the historian focuses on various influences that affect history. In Carl Gustavson's *A Preface to History* and in Jacques Barzun's and Henry Graf's *The Modern Researcher*, the following roles are explained in great detail:

a. Technology
b. Social forces
c. Institutional factor
d. Revolution
e. Individual in history
f. The role of ideas
g. Power
h. International organization
i. Causation
j. Loyalty

There is not enough space to go into great detail about these roles. I highly recommend you read the book by Gustavson if you are interested. If you are still interested, then read Barzun's book.

In Take a Stand!, in writing the questions, I combined the seven different essay types with the various influences of history, making sure that each book contained at least one different essay type, and one different influence of history. The goal is to compel the student to develop all the tools of the historian and to apply them in answering questions.

Learning through a variety of open-ended question types is not only good for the mind, it is enjoyable! The kids will enjoy history more if they have to use different analytical approaches to the history they are studying, and they will have an easier time of remembering what they learned. Teachers enjoy variation in question types, as well, as it makes every class unique.

VI. The Fall of the Roman Empire

Ancient Roman civilization is arguably one of the most important societies for the Western world. Roman contributions in language, law, art, architecture, religion, and other facets of life are still felt in countries such as France and the United States. During its zenith, the Roman Empire spanned as far west as Britannia, east into Asia, north into present-day Germany, and south into Africa. It is hard not to overstate Roman influence in the development of Western civilization.

Like many great civilizations ancient Rome fell.   The Western Roman Empire finally collapsed in A.D. 476. (The Eastern Roman Empire, known as Byzantium, continued until A.D. 1453)

Based on the evidence you research, what were the two most important reasons for the fall of the Roman Empire?   You may choose from the external or internal reasons why Rome fell, but you must choose specific reasons.

Fall of the Roman Empire

A [1]There are many reasons for the fall of the Roman Empire. [2]Both internal and external problems caused its demise.

B [2]British historian Edward Gibbon wrote in *The Decline and Fall of the Roman Empire* that Rome fell because of the destruction of the sanctity of the home, the high divorce rate, the expensive army, the moral decline of the whole society, and the weakening of religious vitality.

C [3]Some hypothesize that lead poisoning hastened Rome's demise. [4]Lead pipes brought water to the cities. [5]The rich drank water and wine from golden cups and their plates were made and decorated with lead. [6]Ingesting lead causes infertility and madness, both traits of a number of Roman rulers.

D [7]Internal problems led to the fall of Rome. [8]Corruption among Roman bureaucrats, politicians, and soldiers weakened the government and army. [9]Disease in Rome wiped out large parts of society. [10]Roman citizens no longer fought and the army relied on foreign, mainly Germanic mercenaries. [11]The mercenaries were not loyal to Rome, but to their generals.

E [12]The Roman Empire also experienced economic troubles. [13]Years of poor harvests on farms resulted in low income and low tax revenue. [14]The Roman government attempted to coin more money to stimulate the economy. [15]However, to do so, it made the coins out of less expensive metals. [16]People didn't respect these Roman coins and demanded higher prices for goods. [17]Inflation led to lower economic activity. [18]The weak economic activity led to less tax revenue. [19]The government borrowed money it couldn't repay, and it couldn't afford security. [20]Bandits robbed people on roads and trade diminished.

F [21]In A.D. 395, after Emperor Theodosius' death, the Roman Empire split in two: The Western Roman Empire had its capital of Rome and the Eastern Roman Empire (also known as the Byzantine Empire) had its capital of Constantinople. [22]Latin was spoken in the West and Greek in the East. [23]These two empires were unable to cooperate and when the Western Roman Empire fell in A.D. 476, the Byzantine Empire did not save it.

G [24]In the fifth century, Asian Huns made war against the Slavic and Germanic peoples in the West and conquered nearly all of Asia and Europe. [25]The Huns, nomadic warriors, pushed the Slavic and Germanic conquests into the crumbling Roman Empire.

H [26]In A.D. 410, Visigoth leader Alaric I captured Rome. [27]It was the first time Rome had been invaded in 800 years! [28]Then, in A.D. 455, the Vandals sacked Rome. [29]The last Roman leader was overthrown by Odoacer, a Germanic leader, who declared himself king of Italy, in A.D. 476.

I [30]The fall of the Western Roman Empire was the end of the ancient world and the beginning of the Medieval Ages. [31]The Eastern Roman Empire continued until 1453.

This passage was taken from Detective World History®, Book One, Copyright by The Critical Thinking Company, with permission.

Bad Emperors of Rome

A [1]The Roman Empire in the West lasted from 27 B.C. to A.D. 476. [2]During that time, Rome was ruled by a number of emperors. [3]Their actions help us understand life in the Roman Empire. [4]Most historians categorize them into two groups: the bad and the good.

B [5]One of the bad emperors was Caligula, (ruled A.D. 37-41). [6]He seized estates of the rich and killed the owners. [7]Caligula insisted he was a god and forced senators and Romans to worship him. [8]He had his wife banished and his father-in-law and cousin were forced to commit suicide. [9]He loved his horse so much he reportedly tried to proclaim his horse consul and priest. [10]Caligula was eventually assassinated.

C [11]Another notorious Roman Emperor was Nero (ruled A.D. 54-68). [12]Nero was accused of fiddling on a violin while a huge fire destroyed much of Rome. [13]He was not in Rome during the fire. [14]He falsely blamed and persecuted the Christians for the fire. [15]Nero spent much of his time pursuing acting and religion. [16]He also spent lavishly. [17]After the fire, he began building Golden House—a palace that would have covered one third of Rome. [18]While away from Rome again, civil war broke out. [19]The Senate condemned him to death, and it's believed he committed suicide.

D [20]Emperor Commodus (A.D. 180-192) loved adoration from the masses and sought attention by actually fighting in the arena as a gladiator. [21]He renamed Rome Colonia Commodia (Colony of Commodus) and thought he was the god Hercules. [22]His advisers had him strangled.

Pages Reprinted from Detective World History®, by John De Gree, with permission from The Critical Thinking Company. All Rights Reserved.

Research Activities

A. Reasons for the Fall of the Roman Empire

1. In A.D. 395, the empire permanently split into two separate entities. This was one reason the Western Roman Empire fell in A.D. 476.
2. _____
3. _____
4. _____
5. _____

B. Explain Your Reasons for the Fall of the Roman Empire

1. The two empires split resources and became weaker.
2. _____
3. _____
4. _____
5. _____

C. Rating the Reasons for the Fall of the Roman Empire

Reasons for the Fall	Rating (1-10)*	Reason for the rating
1.	1.	1.
2.	2.	2.
3.	3.	3.
4.	4.	4.
5.	5.	5.
*A score of 1 means this reason is the most important.		

VII. Teaching with the Socratic Discussion

Once we have taught our students how to analyze history, we will teach them how to discuss and debate. Whereas Socrates used questions to pursue the truth in philosophy, we will use questions to pursue the truth in history. Because much in history is left up to interpretation, this subject is excellent for discussion. Open-ended, interpretive questions are those that are impossible to answer with a simple yes or no, but need explanation. Questions that will stimulate thought and discussion are such as these: "What caused the Roman Empire from persecuting Christians to adopting Christianity as the state religion?" "How did American society change from 1950 to 1990 because of technology?" "What caused the fall of the Soviet Union?" "Compare and contrast the Incas with the Aztecs." "Compare and contrast the reasons Martin Luther and King Henry VIII founded new religions." In their discussions, students will learn that it is possible to look at history from varying vantage points. This exercise in logic trains the mind.

One point that parents need never worry about is whether they themselves know enough to conduct a Socratic discussion in history. Socrates himself noted that the best teacher and most intelligent philosopher is one who knows what he does not know. It is essential that instead of the parent worrying if he knows enough historical information, instead adopts certain habits of thought and of questioning. Once an interpretive question is chosen and the student has researched and formed a perspective the parent needs to ask appropriate questions. Beyond the introductory level of "Who, what, where, when why, how?" however, the parent must ask, "What evidence do you have that supports this?" This is the ultimate question in a discussion in history. If the evidence is weak, then the student's judgment will be weak as well. For how can there be a strong conclusion with weak evidence? The open discussion stimulates the mind to think of other possible conclusions. The parent's primary role is to be the questioner and therefore need not be an expert at each type of history.

The teacher's role in the discussion is not to tell the student what to think, but rather to question and challenge the student's conclusions, forcing the student to continually clarify and defend with historical evidence and sound judgment. If other students are available, the teacher can encourage students to debate each other's ideas, with the intention of arriving at the best possible conclusion together. If there are not other students available, the parent should encourage the student to be able to present a perspective that is contrary to the student's own perspective. In this exercise, the student exercises his mind to view what the opposing side may see. The teacher's goal is to create a scholarly atmosphere where students are free to express their ideas but careful to cite the historical evidence that supports their thesis statement.

The following pages include a set of rules for teachers, one for students. After the student has completed all the research and before the discussion, the teacher should hand this to each student and make sure each student agrees to follow it.

Teacher Guidelines How to Lead the Socratic Discussion in History

1. Have the right frame of mind.
   As the teacher, your role is to encourage discussion and to get your students to explain their answer and reasoning. You are more interested in getting to know who your student is and how he thinks, then giving him information. Researching the history is what your student is supposed to do, not you.

2. Ask the right questions.
   When the student comes forth with his answer, ask him to prove everything.
   "Why do you think this?"
   "What is your evidence?"
   "If you don't have evidence, then maybe you should consider changing your answer."
   "Do you have any historical figures, any dates, and any events that would provide evidence for your answer?"

3. You are the "master" of the process, not the outcome.
   You may have your ideas what the fall of the Roman Empire was, but your role is to challenge the student to come up with his reasons and evidence. If you provide him with your analysis, then he will stop thinking and just wait because you are the teacher who is supposed to be smarter.

4. Let the student Take a Stand!
   The discussion phase is where the student should feel like he is going to shine. Let him shine. Be amazed at good analysis. Support strong use of evidence. Encourage him in his work.

5. Common Errors of Students
   a. Student does not have evidence to back up argument.
   b. Student has one piece of evidence and thinks that that is enough.
   c. Student goes with his "feelings" even though he can't find evidence.
   d. Student is very capable with the spoken word and is used to getting by with a minimum of work.

6. State your perspective and defend it with evidence.
   At the end of the discussion, when all students have spoken, state your judgment and evidence, and let the students comment and challenge you.

Student Rules for a Socratic Discussion in History

1. Each participant has tried their best in researching for the discussion. If no research work has been done, the student cannot participate.

2. The goal of each student is to search for the truth, not "win" the discussion.

3. When others talk, all students will be respectfully silent.

4. To signal the teacher that you want to talk, the student will raise his hand and wait for the teacher to call on him.

5. If a student wants to talk, the teacher will recognize him.

6. In making an assertion, the student will attempt to use historical evidence as support.

7. Unless noted otherwise, students may use notes during the discussion.

8. Students are encouraged to acknowledge good arguments of their peers.

9. The student will make every possible effort to participate in the discussion.

10. If something happens in the discussion that the student thinks should not have, it is up to the student to tell the teacher, either during the discussion or after class.

Copyright© by The Classical Historian 2012. All Rights Reserved. www.classicalhistorian.com

Socratic Discussion Fall of the Roman Empire
Analyze
Class Discussion!

When you share ideas with others, your ideas may be reinforced, rejected, or slightly changed. Listening to your classmates' ideas will help you form your own judgment. If there are other students, interview as many as your teachers instructs you to. Or, discuss with your teacher.

1. What is your name?
2. What do you think were the two main causes of the fall of the Roman Empire?
3. Which evidence do you have that supports what you think?

Reflection
After you have written down all your classmates' responses, think about them and ask yourself the following questions. Write down your answers under your classmates' responses.

1. What do I think of my classmates' answers?
2. Which two reasons are the main reasons why the Roman Empire fell?
3. Did my answers change after I spoke with my classmates?
4. If they changed, why did they and how did they?

You should now have a chance to present your ideas in a classroom discussion. If somebody says something with which you disagree, speak up! In your discussion, you may find out they are actually right and you are wrong. All possible viewpoints should be stated and defended out loud. Test your ideas in class.

VIII. The Writing Process for a One-Paragraph Assignment

To complete the thinking exercise of the historical method, the history essay is a must. Thinking historically requires attributes of patience, perseverance, determination, critical thinking, and open-mindedness. Good writing and the methods that bring students to write well require and support these attributes. Because the historical method calls for a patient, scholarly approach, writing fosters perfectly this attitude. Moreover, when a paper is written, it is easier for the teacher to find if the logic is sound or faulty. It is easier for somebody to pretend when they are speaking, but give them a pen and paper, and the words they write do not disappear. Writing falsehoods are easier to debunk than spoken ones. For the teacher who desires his students become historians, writing is the final and most important step.

For the pre-teen and teenage boy who hates writing because he doesn't know what to write about, historical research gives him all the materials he needs. He has his thesis statement that comes from his answer to the interpretive question. He has his body paragraphs from the historical evidence and analysis that he already has completed. In effect, after the research and debate, the student has in his mind and notes the basics for a good essay.

At the beginning of the year, no matter the age of the student, start with a one-paragraph essay. Once you see how your students write, move up to a five-paragraph essay. From the 8th grade on, I highly recommend that each student write a three to five page essay in the spring, and they then present this essay to the class and parents.

10. Thesis Statement

The **thesis statement** is the main idea or argument of your entire essay. It is your main judgment regarding the essay question, and it should contain words used in the prompt. A thesis statement is not a fact. Instead, it is your judgment of the facts. Because of this, a thesis has to be something with which not everyone will agree. Every thesis will provide an answer to the prompt and a few reasons of support.

Here is an example from the essay question "What were the two most important Roman contributions to world civilizations?" Defend your answer with supporting evidence.

Example 1: The two most important Roman contributions to world civilizations were law and architecture.

This thesis answers the question and provides an outline for the rest of the essay. The reader addresses the question directly and provides general reasons to support his answer. In the essay, the writer will expand on these reasons.

Create two more examples of a thesis based on this first question.

Example 2: _____
_____

Example 3: _____
_____

The Good Thesis Test

If you can answer, "Yes," to these questions, you most likely have a good thesis.

1. Does the thesis address the prompt directly?
2. Does the thesis take a position that I can argue with evidence?
3. Could somebody argue against my thesis statement?

11. Outline for a One-Paragraph Essay

An **outline** helps you organize your thoughts and shows if you have enough evidence to support your thesis statement. An outline does not need to be written in complete sentences, except for the thesis statement and the conclusion. The more evidence you include, the stronger your argument will be.

I. Thesis Statement:
Two most important Roman contributions to world civilizations were language and law.

II. Supporting Evidence:
    1. Latin—mother of languages—French, Portuguese, Romanian, Spanish
    2. Latin and English—"surrender," "champagne"
    3. Roman law—"innocent until proven guilty"
    4. R.L.—"habeas corpus"
    5. Twelve Tables

III. Conclusion:
In conclusion, Roman civilization contributed to the world its rich Latin language and Roman law. With contributions such as the words "surrender" and "champagne," and with legal concepts such as "habeas corpus" and "innocent until proven guilty," many world civilizations are better off because of the Romans.

Following this page are two forms, a "Basic Outline Form for a One-Paragraph Essay," and an "Advanced Outline Form for a One-Paragraph Essay." Your teacher will determine which form you will use. The basic outline is for the beginning historian and the advanced outline is for the more developed and motivated historian.

Basic Outline Form for a One-Paragraph Essay
(Use complete sentences for the thesis statement and the conclusion.)

I. Thesis Statement: _____
_____

    A. Supporting Evidence_____

    B. Supporting Evidence_____

    C. Supporting Evidence_____

II. Conclusion: _____
_____

Advanced Outline Form for a One-Paragraph Essay
(Use complete sentences for the thesis statement and the conclusion.)

I. Thesis Statement: _____
_____

    A. Supporting Evidence_____

    B. Supporting Evidence_____

    C. Supporting Evidence _____

    D. Supporting Evidence _____

    E. Supporting Evidence _____

II. Conclusion: _____
_____

12. Rough Draft for a One-Paragraph Essay

The **rough draft** is the first time that you will explain all the supporting evidence that you use. To do this, take your outline and explain how your evidence supports the thesis statement. Instead of listing your evidence, you will explain its importance. Here is an example of a rough draft of a paragraph. The sentences in bold are those that explain how your evidence supports your topic sentence.

The two most important Roman contributions to world civilizations were language and law. The language of the Romans, Latin, is the mother of many world languages. Spanish, French, Portuguese, and Romanian are all Latin languages. **Just think of it. Millions of people owe their language to the Romans.** English, although a Germanic language, has many Latin roots and is influenced by Latin languages. **Think of the words "surrender" and "champagne." These English words have their beginnings in Latin.** Secondly, Roman law provided a terrific building block for future civilizations. The Justinian Code, created by Emperor Justin, is still in use in France today. Also, the U.S. uses many elements of Roman law, such as the concept "innocent until proven guilty." The idea that a government needs to charge somebody with a crime in order to make an arrest, called "habeas corpus," comes from Roman law. **"Innocent until proven guilty" and "Habeas Corpus" are two legal norms that protect the rights of citizens.** In addition, in the Roman Empire, the law was written and publicly displayed. **All Western societies today have written laws to ensure that leaders try not to take away the rights of the citizens. Even leaders have to follow the law.** In conclusion, Roman civilization contributed to the world its rich Latin language and Roman law. With contributions such as the words "surrender" and "champagne" and legal concepts such as "habeas corpus" and "innocent until proven guilty," many world civilizations are better off because of the Romans.

Basic Rough Draft Form for a One-Paragraph Essay
(Use complete sentences.)

I. Thesis Statement: _____

   A. Supporting Evidence: First of all, _____

Explanation (Explain how this supports the topic sentence): _____

   B. Supporting Evidence: Secondly, _____

Explanation (Explain how this supports the topic sentence): _____

II. Conclusion: In conclusion, _____

Advanced Rough Draft Form for a One-Paragraph Essay
(Use complete sentences.)

I. Thesis Statement: _____
_____

    A. Supporting Evidence: First of all, _____
_____

Explanation (Explain how this supports the topic sentence): _____
_____

    B. Supporting Evidence: Secondly, _____
_____

Explanation (Explain how this supports the topic sentence): _____
_____

    C. Supporting Evidence: Thirdly, _____
_____

Explanation (Explain how this supports the topic sentence): _____
_____

    D. Supporting Evidence: In addition, _____
_____

Explanation (Explain how this supports the topic sentence): _____
_____

    E. Supporting Evidence: Also, _____
_____

Explanation (Explain how this supports the topic sentence): _____
_____

II. Conclusion: _____
_____

13. Revising

After writing the rough draft, it is necessary to revise. Revising involves four steps. Take your essay and perform these four tasks with a red pen in hand.

STEP I   Deletion

Delete dead words: the end, every, just, nice, great, bad, got, everything, getting, so, well, a lot, lots, get, good, some, yours, you, your very

STEP II   Addition

A. Add words, facts, or better descriptions. Imagine you are writing for an adult who does not know the subject well. Explain every point precisely.

B. Use transitions whenever helpful.

To add ideas
further, furthermore, moreover, in addition

To show results
therefore, consequently, as a result

To indicate order
first, second, in addition to

To summarize
to sum up, to summarize, in short

To compare
similarly, likewise, by comparison

Conclusion
In conclusion, to conclude, finally

STEP III   Substitution

Substitute repetitive words and weak-sounding words.

A. Underline the first word in each sentence. If the words are the same, change some of the words.

B. Read your thesis, topic sentences, closers, and conclusion; change words as needed. Is your word choice powerful and effective? Will your essay convince the reader?

STEP IV   Rearrangement

Write sentences that have a variety of beginnings.

Adjective beginnings
Well-equipped, dedicated Union soldiers won the American Civil War.

"ing" words
Riding horses was common among most 1800s Americans.

Prepositional Phrases
Over the vast Pacific Ocean Columbus sailed.

Dependent Clauses
Because of Lincoln, the North did not give up the war effort.

Adverbs - "ly" words
Bravely, Washington led the Continental Army to victory.

Subject + Verb
The boy hit the ball.
The girl kicked the ball.

IX. Advanced Thinking Tools of the Historian
14. Counter Argument

In social studies, many historians have different judgments based on the same evidence. For example, some historians view the Korean War as a success, and others view it as a great loss. These are two very different judgments on U.S. history. These two judgments can be called two perspectives.

When you defend your thesis statement, you should include at least one counter argument. A counter argument is one in which the writer presents an idea that goes against his thesis statement. Then, in that paragraph, the writer shows how this idea is wrong.

For example, imagine if the thesis statement to an essay were, "The Korean War was a monumental failure in U.S. foreign policy." The counter argument paragraph for this thesis should be at the end of the essay, perhaps right before the conclusion paragraph.
Here is an example of a counter argument paragraph:

Some historians may claim that the Korean War was a great success of U.S. foreign policy. They claim that the protection of free Korea kept the Communists in check around the world, and that Americans served a great purpose in dying for other people. Containment, the U.S. policy of keeping world communism to its borders and fighting its expanse, was a false response to communism. World communism was not united, but divided. The Communists in Asia were not united with the Communists in Europe. In fact, the U.S.S.R. and China had troops facing each other at their respective borders because of their distrust. The Warsaw Pact in Europe was a union of European Communist countries to cooperate militarily. Communist China and Communist Korea were not part of this pact. The Communists in Asia were not united with the Communists of Europe, and the conflict in Korea was primarily a regional one, not a global one. U.S. intervention in Korea cost Americans over 50,000 lives, and it was in the end, a precursor to the mistakes of the Vietnam War.

Notice that the beginning of the paragraph above begins with the words "Some historians say." This is because you are presenting an idea that is opposite of yours. In your paragraph, be clear that you think these people are wrong.

15. Analyzing Primary Sources

When you read history and try to analyze it, pay attention to details of the document that tell you important details of the source. These small details can give you incredible insight as to how you should analyze the historical information. Here are a few basic questions to which you should find answers, while you are analyzing historical texts, paintings, or any historical documents.

1. Who wrote (drew, illustrated) it? What position does the writer have? Is the writer a professor, an author of novels? Is the author(s) respected in the field? Did multiple authors prepare the text?

2. Who is (was) the audience? Students? Bookstore customers? Newspaper readers? Magazine readers?

3. When was the text written (drawn/ illustrated)? Was it written during a critical time of history that the text is about? Was it written many years after the time of history it is written about? Are historians more biased about events that happen during our lifetime?

4. Who paid for the text to be written? Is there a chance that the author(s) will be biased because of who is paying for the text?

5. Where was the text written? Was the text written in a place that is in the middle of the historical study the text is about? Is it possible the author can be biased based on where it was written? What country is the author from? Is it possible the country might affect someone's perspective?

6. Who is the publisher? Could the publisher have a bias that might affect the veracity (truth) of the materials?

7. Why was the text written? What was the purpose of the text? Was it meant to be part of a textbook? Was it meant to stir emotions for or against the government?

16. Cause and Effect

Cause and effect is a term that means one event made another event happen. For example, if you push against the pedals of your bicycle, the bicycle moves. In this example, the push against the pedals is the cause and the bicycle moving is the effect.

CAUSE ---→EFFECT
push pedals--→bicycle moves

In social studies, cause and effect usually relates events and people. The relationship is trickier to understand than the above example with the bicycle. Sometimes it is difficult to see causes and effects in history. Here are two examples from American history with which most historians would agree.

CAUSE ---→EFFECT
Japan attacks Pearl Harbor----------------------→the United States enters World War II
the U.S. drops atomic bombs on Japan -------→Japan surrenders

Now, write five causes and effects from history.

Term (Cause)   Effect

1. The North won the Civil War.   1. The U.S. did not break up in 1865.

2. The colonists won the American Revolution.   2._____

3. The Japanese bombed Pearl Harbor.   3._____

4. The U.S.A. dropped atomic bombs on Japan.   4._____

5._____   5._____

17. Compare and Contrast

To **compare** means to look at two or more objects and recognize what they have in common. To **contrast** means to look at two or more objects and recognize what they have different from each other.

Try to compare and contrast World War I with World War II.

World War I		World War II
Differences	**Similarities**	**Differences**

X. The Writing Process for a Five-Paragraph Assignment

A. Thesis Statement for a Five-Paragraph Essay

The **thesis statement** is the main idea or argument of your entire essay. It is your judgment regarding the essay question and it should contain words used in the prompt. A thesis statement is not a fact. Instead, it is your judgment of the evidence. Because of this, a thesis has to be something with which not everyone will agree. In a five-paragraph essay you should list three pieces of evidence in your thesis in order to provide the reader with an outline of your essay.

Here is an example from the essay question "What made unifying ancient China so difficult?" Because this essay requires a five-paragraph response, the student will need three supporting pieces of evidence for the body paragraphs. These three should be included in the thesis.

Example 1: Unifying ancient China was so difficult because of geography, language, and foreign invasions.

This thesis answers the question and provides an outline for paragraphs two, three, and four. Paragraph two will detail information about foreign policy, paragraph three about domestic affairs, and paragraph four about presidential elections.

Create two more thesis statements for a five-paragraph essay based on this question.

Example 2: _____   _____
Example 3: _____   _____

The Good Thesis Test

If you can answer, "Yes," to these questions, you most likely have a good thesis for a five-paragraph essay:

1. Does my thesis address the prompt directly?
2. Does my thesis take a position that I can argue with evidence?
3. Could somebody argue against my thesis statement?

B. Outlining and Writing a Rough Draft For an Essay

After all the research has been completed, the writer must spend time organizing his thoughts. This is best done through the exercise of outlining. Outlining the essay provides the writer with a structure to follow, and also shows him if he has enough evidence to support his thesis. Writing a rough draft for a history paper means to take an outline and make a first attempt at writing the essay. The basic difference between the outline and the rough draft is that the former is written for the writer to understand and the latter is written for the reader to understand. In the following lesson on the next page, the student needs to fill in the blanks. If he is unable to fill in the spots left for "Supporting Evidence," then he must reassess whether he has enough evidence to argue his thesis, if he should change his thesis, or if he should research more.

Outline and rough draft forms give students a specific idea of what they should include in their essays. There are two sets of forms: basic and advanced. The basic form is meant for the beginning social studies writer, the advanced form for the more experienced. The main difference between these two forms is the amount of supporting evidence each requires. The basic form requires only two, whereas the advanced has space for up to five. Student needs and the teacher's prerogative decide how many pieces of supporting evidence are needed for a good essay. Some students will want to include as many as possible, however, in an effort to write the strongest essay.

B. Outlining a Five-Paragraph Essay

An **outline** is a skeleton for your essay. Here, you organize your essay before writing it out in complete sentences. If you have a framework first, it will be fairly easy to write the essay. Below is an explanation of writing an outline for a five-paragraph essay.

A. First Paragraph: For the first paragraph, write down the thesis and list the three topics that will be your body paragraphs.

B. Body Paragraphs

1. Organize your paragraphs into topics by following the order you wrote in the thesis. Your thesis should have listed three topics. The first will be the topic of your second paragraph, the second the topic of your third, and the third the topic of your fourth paragraph.

2. You do not need to write complete sentences for your outline. It is enough to write the topics of each paragraph and to list the supporting evidence for your topic sentence in your outline. You will add more information when you write your draft.

3. Document each source! Write the author's last name and the page where you found this information.

C. Conclusion

The conclusion is the place where you restate your thesis and your topic sentences. You will convince the reader better by a reminder at the end what your essay was all about. After the restatements, finish the essay with strong words supporting your thesis.

Basic Outline Form for a Five-Paragraph Essay
(Use complete sentences for the thesis, topic sentences, closers, and conclusion.)

Paragraph I.
Thesis Statement: _____
_____

Paragraph II.
I. Topic Sentence: _____
_____
      A. Supporting Evidence: _____
      B. Supporting Evidence: _____
II. Closer: _____
_____Write the source: _____

Paragraph III.
I. Topic Sentence: _____
_____
      A. Supporting Evidence: _____
      B. Supporting Evidence: _____
II. Closer: _____
_____Write the source: _____

Paragraph IV.
I. Topic Sentence: _____
_____
      A. Supporting Evidence: _____
      B. Supporting Evidence: _____
II. Closer: _____
_____Write the source: _____

Paragraph V. Conclusion
I. Restate thesis statement: _____
_____
II. Strong statement that shows how the topic sentences support the thesis: _____
_____

Advanced Outline Form for a Five-Paragraph Essay
(Use complete sentences for the thesis, topic sentences, closers, and conclusion.)

Paragraph I.
Thesis Statement: _____
_____

Paragraph II.
I. Topic Sentence: _____
_____
     A. Supporting Evidence:_____
     B. Supporting Evidence: _____
     C. Supporting Evidence:_____
     D. Supporting Evidence:_____
     E. Supporting Evidence:_____
II. Closer: _____
_____Write the source:_____

Paragraph III.
I. Topic Sentence: _____
_____
     A. Supporting Evidence:_____
     B. Supporting Evidence: _____
     C. Supporting Evidence:_____
     D. Supporting Evidence:_____
     E. Supporting Evidence:_____
II. Closer: _____
_____Write the source:_____

Paragraph IV. Use another page or the back of this paper.

Paragraph V. Conclusion
I. Restate thesis statement: _____
_____

II. Strong statement that shows how the topic sentences support the thesis:_____
_____
_____

2. Rough Draft for a Five-Paragraph Essay

a. Introductory Paragraph
The social studies essay begins directly with the thesis. Following the thesis is a brief explanation of the main topics that will be written in detail in the body paragraphs. Below is an example from the essay question "Why did the Communists have success in Russia?"

The Communists had success in Russia because of the Russian failures in World War I, the bold leadership and dynamic personality of Vladimir Lenin, and the transformation of Russian society from a medieval peasant culture to a modern, technological state. In 1917, Russia faced a number of very difficult challenges. The Central Powers (Germany, Austro-Hungarian empire, the Ottoman empire) were clearly winning the war. Disaffection with the war caused many Russians to turn to anti-war leaders. Lenin was anti-war, but he was seen as a dynamic and forceful leader. Lastly, Russian society resembled the medieval world of serf and master, and it was in the midst of great social upheaval. These three reasons led Russia to the arms of the Communists, who promised radical changes.

b. The Body
The body of your essay is where you present your evidence to prove your thesis. In these paragraphs, you will present your evidence and explain how it supports the topic sentence. An example of this is found in Skill #10, Rough Draft for a One-Paragraph Essay. Keep the order of your arguments the same as the order of mention in the thesis. Attempt to order the events chronologically.

c. Conclusion
In this paragraph, you need to restate your thesis, tie the topic sentences of your body paragraphs to the thesis, and leave the reader with the strongest evidence that supports your argument. Your job is to convince the reader that your position is correct. Write strongly!

Following this page are two forms—one basic and one advanced—to help you develop your rough draft.

Basic Rough Draft Form for a Five-Paragraph Essay
(Use complete sentences. Use the back when you need space.)

Paragraph I.
Thesis Statement:_____
_____

Paragraph II.
Topic Sentence: _____
_____

A. Supporting Evidence: First of all, _____
_____

Explanation (Explain how the evidence supports the thesis): _____
_____

B. Supporting Evidence: Secondly,_____
_____

Explanation (Explain how the evidence supports the thesis): _____
_____

II. Closer: In conclusion, _____
_____

Paragraphs III and IV. Follow the structure of Paragraph II.

Paragraph V. Conclusion
I. Restate thesis statement: _____
_____
_____

II. Strong statement that shows how the topic sentences support the thesis: _____
_____

Copyright© by The Classical Historian 2012. All Rights Reserved. www.classicalhistorian.com

Advanced Rough Draft Form for a Five-Paragraph Essay
(Use complete sentences.)

Paragraph I.
Thesis Statement: _____
_____

Paragraph II.
I. Topic Sentence: _____
_____

A. Supporting Evidence: First of all, _____
_____

Explanation (Explain how this supports the thesis):_____
_____

B. Supporting Evidence: Secondly, _____
_____

Explanation (Explain how this supports the thesis): _____
_____

C. Supporting Evidence: Thirdly, _____
_____

Explanation (Explain how this supports the thesis):_____
_____

D. Supporting Evidence: In addition, _____
_____

Explanation (Explain how this supports the thesis): _____
_____

E. Supporting Evidence: Furthermore, _____
_____

Explanation (Explain how this supports the thesis): _____
_____

II. Closer: _____
_____

Paragraphs III and IV. Follow the same structure as above.

Paragraph V. Conclusion
I. Restate thesis statement: _____
_____
_____

II. Strong statement that shows how the topic sentences support the thesis:
_____
_____

Chapter XI. Grading Essays

Grading papers is the most tiresome and time-consuming job a teacher can have. This misery is made worse when the average class size in some schools is 40 students. Teachers with six classes of 40 students each would have to spend 240 minutes, or six hours, to grade all students' papers at a rate of one paper per minute. This is obviously impossible. The tactics below will facilitate the grading process, if you are a classroom teacher. If you are not a classroom teacher, and can spend much time on each paper, skip to #1. Grading Papers One at a Time, located after the next few paragraphs.

Grading papers involves an element of individual prerogative on the part of the grader. Teachers attempt to create grading rubrics to make the process as transparent and unbiased as possible. However, every teacher has certain areas of focus. As a general rule, I do not focus primarily on grammatical errors, unless the mistakes take away from understanding the students' arguments. This suits my purposes as a history teacher using essays as a tool to understand and remember the past. It may not suit your purposes perfectly. Knowing this, please keep in mind that my suggestions are not laws written in stone. These suggestions are from a history teacher who is mainly concerned with students learning analytical skills and applying them to history. You may find that you won't agree with everything that I recommend, or that I am too easy on issues of grammar and style.

Sometimes, the best ideas come from those who do not have a terrific command of language. I recall an excellent professor in political science who spoke English with poor grammar, but taught his content extremely well. It would have been better for the students if the professor would have spoken English better. However, this professor was able to communicate more than well enough to teach us the content.

Below is a list of ideas to save time in grading many essays. Before collecting the work, have students underline their thesis statement in blue ink, the evidence used in red, the evidence explained in pencil, and the conclusion—optionally— in another color. This will facilitate your grading. Refer to the list below for more time-saving ideas in grading papers:

1. Painstakingly teach the social studies literacy skills until the students fully understand them.
2. Work with the students thoroughly on all portions of the assignment. Check for understanding on their prewriting activities.
3. Grade only the outline.
4. Grade only the thesis statement.
5. Grade only the evidence used.
6. Grade only the evidence explained.
7. Grade only the conclusion.
8. Lead a writing workshop where students grade each other and make corrections in red pen on their classmates' papers. Lead the students to use the *Take a Stand!*™ grading rubrics, which are included in the student books. Then, make the students rewrite their papers.
9. Have students present their paper in class. Have the student hand you the essay, and let him present his argument to the class. Grade his presentation.

10. Give a multiple-choice exam and let the student use his essay to help him write the test.

Rotate your use of the above strategies. For example, for one paper, grade only the thesis statement and for the next, grade the evidence. Keep rotating your strategy for grading essays until the end of the year comes. For the last essay, I highly recommend students join a small team and do work together, making a final presentation during the last week of school. You grade only the presentation, and all students are busily working on something worthwhile.

Grading Papers One at a Time

Optimally, you will have time to thoroughly grade papers. To do so, follow the *Take a Stand!* grading rubrics. Below are the grading rubrics for a one paragraph and a five paragraph essay, with a short description of each category. This grading scale is based on the four-point scale used by the California Department of Education. To locate this on the web, go to www.cde.ca.gov/ta/tg/hs/elateacherguide.asp and choose the link *Appendices*. This site offers an abundance of information on grading essays. Refer to this site for specific grading explanations and essay examples.

A. One-Paragraph Essay Grading Rubric

    4   Exceeds Standards
    3   Meets Standards
    2   Approaching Standards
    1   Below Standards
    0   Nonexistent

                                                              Y/N

I.   Thesis Statement:
      Does it persuasively answer the question?
                                      Score _____

II.   Evidence Used:
      Are two or more relevant pieces of evidence used?
                                      Score _____

III. Evidence Explained
      Is the evidence explained correctly and persuasively?
                                      Score _____

IV. Conclusion:
      Does the evidence strengthen the topic sentence?
                                      Score _____

V.   Prewriting Activities
      Are all prewriting activities included and attached
      to the final?
                                      Score _____

              Total Addition of Scores = _____
                                          <u>X 5</u>
                          Score = _____

Spelling or Grammatical Errors   -_____
Missing Prewriting Work   -_____

                        Final Score = _____

Grading Categories for the One Paragraph Essay

I. **Thesis Statement:** Does it persuasively answer the question?
The **thesis statement** is the main idea or argument of the entire essay. It is the writer's main judgment regarding the essay question, and it should contain words used in the prompt. A thesis statement is not a fact. Instead, it is the writer's judgment of the facts. Because of this, a thesis has to be something with which not everyone will agree. Every thesis will provide pieces of evidence in order to provide the reader with a general outline of the essay.

II. **Evidence Used:** Are two or more relevant pieces of evidence used?
Supporting evidence refers to everything used to support the thesis that can be verified. It is important for the writer to show that the judgment is based on factual pieces of evidence, and not on opinion. Names, dates, and events are used to support the thesis statement. **Evidence Explained:** Is the evidence explained correctly and persuasively? **Judgment** in social studies means a person's evaluation of facts. For example, consider the following two sentences. The French Revolution began in 1789. This year was very important for France. The fact in these sentences is that the French Revolution began in 1789. The judgment is that this year was important for France. Judgment is different from opinion because judgment is based on fact whereas opinion is not. Good judgment is very persuasive but bad judgment is not.

III. **Conclusion:** Does the evidence strengthen the topic sentences?
The **conclusion** ties the evidence presented in the essay back to the thesis statement. It is the writer's last chance to present how the evidence supports the thesis statement. In a one-paragraph essay, the conclusion can be one sentence, but it may be more. In the conclusion, the student should not introduce new pieces of supporting evidence but rather should provide mainly analysis.

IV. **Prewriting Activities:** Are all prewriting activities included and attached to the final? For this category, the teacher is grading primarily the effort of the student.

V. **The Unwritten Category:** Do grammatical or spelling errors detract from the reader's understanding? Total possible points to be deducted here is up to teacher discretion. I recommend that for the first few assignments grading in this category be lenient. Our main goal is to promote critical thinking, speaking, and writing. If the spelling and grammar errors do not keep the reader from understanding the content, the grader should tread lightly on deducting for these mistakes.

The Five-Paragraph Essay

The five-paragraph is the standard for essay tests in secondary schools. Once a student can master this essay, all writing assignments will be made easier throughout the student's academic career, including at the university level. Below are two examples of five-paragraph essays based on a question from this book.

B. Five-Paragraph Essay Grading Rubric

Grading Scale
4   Exceeds Standards
3   Meets Standards
2   Approaching Standards
1   Below Standards
0   Nonexistent

Paragraph I.   Yes/No
A. Thesis: Does it answer the question and provide organizational structure? _____
B. Interest?   Does it grab the interest of the reader? _____
                         Score: _____

Paragraph II.
A. Topic Sentence: Does it provide a strong statement supporting the thesis? _____
B. Evidence: 1. Is evidence used to support the topic sentence? _____
                 2. Is the evidence explained clearly and in detail? _____
C. Closer: Does the closer convincingly link the paragraph's evidence with the topic sentence? _____
                         Score: _____

Paragraph III.
A. Topic Sentence: Does it provide a strong statement supporting the thesis? _____
B. Evidence: 1. Is evidence used to support the topic sentence? _____
                 2. Is the evidence explained clearly and in detail? _____
C. Closer: Does the closer convincingly link the paragraph's evidence with the topic sentence? _____
                         Score: _____

Paragraph IV.
A. Topic Sentence: Does it provide a strong statement supporting the thesis? _____
B. Evidence: 1. Is evidence used to support the topic sentence? _____
                 2. Is the evidence explained clearly and in detail? _____
C. Closer: Does the closer convincingly link the evidence with the topic sentence? _____
                         Score: _____

Paragraph V.
A. Restating Topic Sentences: Are the topic sentences in II, III, IV restated? _____
B. Closer: Does the Closer persuasively show that the main ideas of paragraphs II, III, and IV strongly support the thesis? _____

                         Score: _____ X 5 = _____
                 Spelling or Grammatical Errors -_____
                 Missing Prewriting Work -_____

                 Total Score _____

C. Student Sample Essays and Grades

Below are sample student essays with corresponding grades and teacher notes. For a teacher of history, the best instruction on how to grade papers comes with experience. The more papers you grade, the more you will know what to look for. The following essays are similar to those that could be written by students in secondary school education.

From Ancient Civilizations: The One-Paragraph Essay

Below are two sample one-paragraph essays that could be written by a sixth grader. Spelling and grammatical mistakes are found in these samples to demonstrate imperfect essays. Note: When I graded these papers, I graded them primarily on their content instead of grammar. It is possible for our scores to vary, but the variance in grading shouldn't be too great. For example, one teacher may grade an essay to be an "A" and another grade the same paper a "B". But, when the grading difference is more than two grades different, then usually this means that one of the graders is being too strict, or one is being too mean. I have to confess, that after many years in the classroom, I may have become too easy of a grader for essays.

Question: Name the two most important contributions to the world from the ancient civilizations of Mesopotamia, Egypt, and Kush.

Student Essay #1

"Mesopotamia egypt and kush

The two most important contributation to the world made by ancient cyvalization of Mesopotamia and kush and Egypt is wheel from sumeria and the boat from kush. The wheel made them travel to seterant places. It took them days to go to a place. They were happy because it didn't take them month to get there. They use thre boats for sertant things. They could use the boat for a table or they could ude it to make their house to sleep in. When they could make fire is that they could cut it from the boat and make fire. The most important constributiontrons to the world is a wheel for summeria and the boat from Kush.

Student Essay #2

"Mesopotamia, Egypt, and Kush"

The two most important contributions to the world from ancient Mesopotamia, Egypt, and Kush were writing from Phoenicia and written laws from the Babylonian Empire. Before Phoenicia, the Mesopotamian civilization of Sumeria had created cuneiform. This written language consisted of symbols that represented something or a sound. Sumerians had over 700 of these symbols. Phoenicia, however, created an alphabet of 22 letters. The alphabet was superior to the symbols as it was simpler to express an idea by creating words. The Latin alphabet comes from the Phoenician alphabet. Hammurabi's Code from the Babylonian Empire was the second most important contribution from Mesopotamia, Egypt, and Kush. King Hammurabi (1792-1750 B.C.) had laws written for his empire. His laws created a society with uniform codes. This system made it safer for all citizens, as all knew their respective rights. While some laws favored the rich and powerful, Hammurabi's Code created a civilization of laws, not just of men. This means that if a strong person tried to abuse his fellow citizens, a weaker person could turn to Hammurabi's Code for protection. In addition, this code protected the rights of patients and women and punished dishonest businessmen. In conclusion, the two most important contributions from ancient Mesopotamia, Egypt, and Kush were writing from Phoenicia and written laws from the Babylonian Empire.

Before looking below, use the Grading Rubric to assess the two essays! Then, compare how you assessed the papers with how Mr. De Gree did. It is alright if you disagree with Mr. De Gree, as long as you don't fail a paper when he passed it.

Grading Notes for Student Essay #1

I. Thesis Statement: Grade: 2.5 Approaching Standards

This student answers the question directly and correctly writes which civilization contributed the wheel and boat. However, spelling and grammatical errors make it difficult for the reader to understand the thesis statement.

II. Evidence Used: Grade: 2 Approaching Standards

The student attempts to explain with common sense how the contributions of the wheel and the boat are important. In a short paragraph with this somewhat simple topic, this is not necessarily a bad idea. However, because of the spelling and grammatical errors, the writer appears not to understand the topic well. It would have been helpful if the writer used a specific example of how Sumeria used the wheel and how Kush used the boat. On what river did the citizens of Kush sail? Did Sumeria use the wheel for war? The writer should have addressed these issues.

III. Evidence Explained: Grade: 2.5 Approaching Standards

The author makes an attempt to explain the reasons behind his two choices, but he really does not use any arguments in history to prove his point.

IV. Conclusion: Grade: 2.5 Approaching Standards

The writer has a concluding sentence, but it does not make sense. "A wheel for Sumeria" is incorrect as the wheel came *from* Sumeria. This conclusion is sloppy.

V. Prewriting Activities: Grade: 3 Meets Standards

This student completed all prewriting assignments, but did not attempt to go beyond basic requirements. For example, this student used only the minimum amount of sources the teacher required.

VI. The Unwritten Category: Grade: -10

The essay contains a substantial number of spelling and grammatical errors. These problems require that a lesser grade be assigned than the writer otherwise would have received.

Grade for Student Essay #1

Thesis:	2.5 x	5 = 12.5
Evidence Used:	2 x	5 = 10
Evidence Explained:	2.5 x	5 = 12.5
Conclusion:	2.5 x	5 = 12.5
Prewriting Activities	3 x	5 = 15
Sub Total:		62.5
Spelling and Grammatical Errors:		-10
Total Grade: F		52.5

Grading Notes for Student Essay #2

I. Thesis Statement: Grade: 4 Exceeds Standards

This student answers the question directly and correctly writes which civilization contributed the wheel and boat. It is a matter of teacher's prerogative to score this a 3 or a 4. For a one-paragraph essay, I prefer scoring a logically sound thesis statement with a 4 rather than a 3.

II. Evidence Used: Grade: 4   Exceeds Standards

There is an abundance of supporting evidence in this one paragraph, and there are no historical errors.

III. Evidence Explained: Grade: 4   Exceeds Standards

The student analyzes the importance of the contribution of the alphabet and of Hammurabi's Code. This analysis brings out the importance of these two contributions.

IV. Conclusion: Grade: 4   Exceeds Standards

The student restates the thesis statement. As with the thesis statement in this essay, the teacher could score this a 3 or a 4. For a one-paragraph essay, this conclusion earns a 4.

V. Prewriting Activities: Grade: 4   Meets Standards

This student completed all prewriting assignments and used more sources than the teacher required.

VI. The Unwritten Category: Grade: Nothing subtracted

The essay does not contain any errors that detract from understanding the content, and is interesting to read.

Total Grade for Essay #2:   A+   100

Five-Paragraph Essay

Question: What were the two most important causes of the greatness of the Roman Republic?

"The Roman Republic Survived"

The two most important causes of the greatness of the Roman Republic were the Roman government and the Roman people. The Roman Republic existed from 509 to approximately 60 B.C., but its influence can be felt today. This four hundred year republic no longer exists, of course, but the ideas, philosophies, stories, and sciences of ancient Rome influence our society to a great deal. Though the Roman Republic can be found in the history books, we can also see it surviving today.

The government of the Roman Republic was one reason for its greatness. The Roman Republic was split into three main powers: a law-making body, an executive, and a judiciary. The Assemblies made law, two Consuls enforced the law and acted as dictators during war, and Praetors were judges. By separating the powers of government into three branches, the Romans ensured that not one person, or one branch of government, could ever act tyrannical. Each of the two Consuls had veto power over the other. This ensured that one Consul could not easily become a tyrant. In addition, the main laws of the Roman Republic were written and on public display. These laws were called the Twelve Tables. The Twelve Tables ensured that one law ruled all of the republic, and that all citizens had rights. The Twelve Tables also established respect for written laws. Roman citizens chose leaders of the government. This made the government responsible to the Roman citizens. The American system of government emulated the Roman Republic's government in many ways. The United States has three branches of government. Citizens choose America's leaders. Even though the Roman Republic ceased in 60 B.C., the republican ideas live today in the United States of America, and in other countries as well.

The Roman people were a second cause of the greatness of the Roman Republic. Cincinnatus lived in the fifth and sixth century B.C. He exemplifies early Roman characteristics: hard working, humble, and unselfish. Foreign invaders threatened ancient Rome. Roman leaders asked Cincinnatus, a farmer, to become dictator of Rome to lead in the defense of his homeland. Cincinnatus agreed, even though it meant great sacrifice to his family. After Cincinnatus defeated the enemy, he quickly stepped down from power and went back to his farm. Cincinnatus' actions show that he was not interested in keeping power to himself. He preferred taking care of his family, and the hard work of farm life, to that of the glorious life of a military hero. It is Romans such as Cincinnatus who made Rome great.

The influence of the Roman Republic can be felt today, especially in the United States. American government follows many Roman practices. The United States has three branches, just like the Roman Republic had. In the United States, there is the legislative branch (Congress), the executive branch (President), and the judiciary branch (Courts). These three branches are very similar to the Assemblies, the Consuls, and the Praetors of the Roman Republic. In addition, many of our country's monuments and government buildings are built in a style similar to the architecture of ancient Rome. The U.S. Capitol and the White House are constructed in neo-classical architecture. Statues of George Washington exist which show him as a Roman leader, with a toga. In conclusion, though the Roman Republic ended, its influence is still seen today.

The greatness of Rome can be attributed to two main causes: government and people. The Roman Republic had a government that enabled citizens to have freedom. By splitting the power of government into three branches, the Roman Republic made sure that not one man would take over. Also, the people of Rome created a great society. Rome's influence can be seen today in the United States.

Before moving on, use the Grading Rubric to assess the essay! Then, compare how you assessed the papers with how Mr. De Gree did. It is alright if you disagree with Mr. De Gree, as long as you don't fail a paper when he passed it.

Grading Notes for Student Essay "The Roman Republic Survived"
Paragraph I.   **Thesis Statement and Interest**
Grade: 3.5   **Meets Standards**
The thesis statement addresses the prompt directly and clearly. The writer introduces the main topics of the essay in an exciting and convincing manner. However, the author writes that "the ideas, philosophies, stories, and sciences of ancient Rome influence our society to a great deal." There is nothing in the essay that supports this statement regarding stories and sciences.
Paragraph II.   **Topic Sentence, Evidence, Closer**
Grade: 4   **Exceeds Standards**
The student uses a large amount of supporting evidence, explains it clearly, and has a strong closer.
Paragraph III.   **Topic Sentence, Evidence, Closer**
Grade: 2   **Approaching Standards**
Paragraph three does not mention the year Cincinnatus became dictator, nor do we know the name of the invading army. While the paragraph explains Cincinnatus' actions well, it lacks historical evidence.
Paragraph IV.   **Topic Sentence, Evidence, Closer**

Grade: 3.5   **Meets Standards**

The author convincingly writes how the government of the Roman Republic influenced the American Republic. Regarding architecture, the author could have done a more detailed description of Roman architecture. The author uses the term neo-classical architecture without letting the reader know what this is.

Paragraph V   **Restating Thesis Statement and Closer**

V.   **Conclusion:**   **Grade:**   3   **Meets Standards**

The conclusion does not mention Cincinnatus, The author also leaves out any mention of architecture, though it is part of the body paragraphs.

Spelling or Grammatical Errors?

There are no errors that detract from the content of the essay.

Grade for "The Roman Republic Survived"

Paragraph I.	3.5 x 5 =	17.5
Paragraph II.	4 x 5 =	20
Paragraph III.	2 x 5 =	10
Paragraph IV.	3.5 x 5 =	17.5
Paragraph V.	3 x 5 =	15
Total	**B-**	**80**

Essays from Medieval Civilizations
The One-Paragraph Essay

Below are two sample one-paragraph essays that could be written by a seventh grade student. Spelling and grammatical mistakes are found in these samples to demonstrate imperfect essays.

Student Essay #1

Question: What were the two most important reasons for the fall of the Roman Empire?

"The Fall"

     The two most important reasons for the fall of the Roman Empire is because they weren't strong enough and because the barbarians. The Roman Empire was getting weaker and weaker over the years. After Julius Caesar left, Rome was never the same. Generals fought each other, and people outside of rome got stronger. Germans came in and caused problems. Secondly, the barbarians invaded the roman empire and took over. In conclusion, the Roman Empire fell because they got weaker and the barbarians got stronger.

Student Essay #2

Question: Why did the Byzantine Empire survive when the Roman Empire fell in 476 A.D.?

"Survival"

     The Eastern Roman Empire (also known as Byzance or the Byzantine Empire) continued after the fall of the Western Roman Empire because of its location, its superior weaponry, and its respect for law and order. The Byzantine Empire and the Western Roman Empire had been united as one, until Emperor Theodosius I died in A.D. 395. At his death, he split the empire in two, bequeathing one half to each of his two sons. It is believed Theodosius I thought the empire would be easier to govern and defend if it were split in two. The location of Constantinople, capital city of Byzantium, enabled its citizens to build protective barriers that kept it safe from invasion for over 1000 years. Also, Byzantium was farther away from Germanic barbarian tribes such as the Ostrogoths, Visigoths, Vandals, and Franks, and did not feel the pressure these tribes placed on the Western Roman Empire from the north. Asian warriors led by "Attila the Hun" also threatened Rome. In addition, Byzantium developed more advanced weaponry against invasion. "Greek Fire" was an effective Byzantine weapon. Hurled at an enemy, Greek Fire made its target burn. If you tried to put it out with water, it only spread. Lastly, Byzance had a strong respect for law and order. Emperor Justinian worked to gather all the best laws of Rome and wrote a complete set of governmental codes, known as the Justinian Code. Byzantium also had a secret police and spies, which did not tolerate any threat to the government. In conclusion, the Eastern Roman Empire, also known as Byzantium, outlasted the Western Roman Empire by nearly 1000 years, finally succumbing to the Seljuk Turks in A.D. 1453 because of its location, its superior weaponry, and its respect of law and order, Byzantium endured for many years.

Grading Notes for Student Essay #1 "The Fall"

I.   Thesis Statement: Grade: 2   Approaching Standards
The student uses a pronoun and a phrase inappropriately, creating a poorly written thesis statement. He writes, "because they weren't strong," probably referring to the Roman Empire. The reader has to take a guess with this link, however. Furthermore, "because the barbarians" is an incomplete idea.

II.   Evidence Used: Grade: 1   Below Standards
There is practically no evidence provided. It appears the student did not work in researching for this assignment.

III.   Evidence Explained: Grade: 1   Below Standards
Because the evidence is so small, it is impossible for this essayist to score high in this category.

IV.   Conclusion: Grade: 2   Approaching Standards
This conclusion is a complete idea, but it is not based on any evidence the writer used. Also, the use of the pronoun "they" is again inappropriately used although it does tie in to the writer's thesis statement.

V.   Prewriting Activities: Grade: 2   Approaching Standards
This student completed all assignments, but the effort was obviously minimal.

VI.   The Unwritten Category: Grade: -5
Mistakes in grammar hurt this student's essay. For example, subject-verb agreement is lacking in the thesis statement, and capitalization is faulty with "rome" and "roman empire."

Grade for "The Fall"

Thesis:	2 x 5 = 10
Evidence Used:	1 x 5 = 5
Evidence Explained:	1 x 5 = 5
Conclusion:	2 x 5 = 10
Prewriting Activities	2 x 5 = 10
Sub Total:	50
Spelling and Grammatical Errors:	-5
Total Grade: F	**45**

Grade Notes for Student Essay #2 "Survival"

I.   Thesis Statement: Grade: 4   Exceeds Standards
This thesis statement directly and clearly responds to the prompt and provides reasons for the answer.

II.   Evidence Used: Grade: 4   Exceeds Standards
The writer uses a large amount of historical evidence to support the thesis. The mention of names, dates, and places, and the use of the legal document the Justinian Code and the weapon of Greek Fire go a long way in convincing the reader that the author has a strong historical argument.

III.   **Evidence Explained:**   Grade: 4   **Exceeds Standards**

After each piece of evidence, the author goes into detail explaining how the evidence supports the thesis statement.

IV.   **Conclusion:**   Grade: 3   **Meets Standards**

The last sentence of the paragraph contains a small error that confuses the author's meaning. The author probably meant to write that Byzantium survived because of its location, its superior weaponry, and its respect of law and order. However, it currently reads that the Seljuks conquered Bzantium because of its location, its superior weaponry, and its respect of law and order.

V.   **Prewriting Activities: Grade:**   4   **Exceeds Standards**

This student's research shows that extra research was conducted. Many sources were used.

VI.   **The Unwritten Category:**   Grade: 3   **Meets Standards**

Because of the last sentence, this student could not score a perfect 4. Other than this, there are no mistakes that detract from understanding the content.

Grade for "The Fall"

Thesis:		4 x 5 = 20
Evidence Used:	4 x 5 = 20	
Evidence Explained:		4 x 5 = 20
Conclusion:		3 x 5 = 15
Prewriting Activities:		4 x 5 = 20
Sub Total:		95
Spelling and Grammatical Errors:		-2
Total Grade:	A	**93**

The Three-Paragraph Essay

For sixth-graders, I recommend stopping at the three-paragraph essay. The main goal of "Take a Stand!" is to promote critical thinking, reading, discussing, and writing. These goals are accomplished well in small essays. In concentrating on shorter assignments, the sixth-grader can spend most of their time analyzing history. For seventh graders, I recommend the three-paragraph essay as a bridge between the one and five-paragraph essay. For all other grade levels, the five-paragraph essay can be written after writing the one-paragraph essay. The three-paragraph assignment is an extension of the one-paragraph essay, and it helps the younger student grow accustomed to writing longer papers, but may not be necessary for the older or more advanced student. While the student book does not specifically teach the three-paragraph essay, you may do so by explaining to the student that the thesis statement and conclusion will be in more detail and they will be in separate paragraphs.

Student Essay #1

Question: Under the Shoguns, was medieval Japan violent or peaceful, open or closed, culturally rich or poor?

"Medieval Japan"

During Medieval Japan, from approximately A.D. 1185-1867, powerful military leaders called shoguns created a violent, closed, and culturally rich society. Shoguns were originally enforcers of the law under the emperors, but over time became the ultimate authority in Japan. For nearly seven hundred years, shoguns ruled Japan with an iron fist.

Shogun society in medieval Japan was violent, closed, and culturally rich. First of all, shoguns were powerful military generals who ruled Japan like dictators. Shoguns controlled not only the military, but also the country's finances, courts, and official appointments. Under the shoguns, warriors, known as samurai, ruled farms like European knights. The samurai warrior was so dedicated to honor and courage that if he dishonored himself in some way he would commit suicide by stabbing himself in the abdomen and heart (seppuku). During the time of the shoguns, Japan fought a civil war that lasted over 100 years (c.1475–1603). Medieval Japan was based on the power of the samurai and shogun, and this time was a violent period for Japan. Secondly, medieval Japan was a closed society, primarily to ideas and people outside of Asia. French Catholic missionary Francis Xavier arrived in Japan in 1549. Very quickly, there was a large number of Japanese Catholics, with at least 250,000 by 1610. However, the Tokugawa Shogunate distrusted the westerners, and persecuted all Christians by either killing them or driving them out of the country. The Catholic Church was allowed back in Japan only after World War II. Lastly, even though medieval Japan was mainly a closed society, it was culturally rich. In theater, "No" plays were produced. Artistic tea ceremonies were cultivated. And, artistic Japanese gardens became common. In conclusion, medieval Japan was violent, closed, and culturally rich.

    To say that medieval Japan was violent, closed, and culturally rich is to say that this country was very similar to other medieval world cultures. Japan's reliance on the shoguns and samurai is similar to Europe's reliance on a fighting king and the landed knights. The fact that Japan was closed is very similar to the situation in central Europe, where ideas of the outside were fought with a vengeance. However, Japan's cultural activities may put it a step ahead other world cultures during the medieval times.

Grade Notes for Essay #1 "Medieval Japan"

I.   **Thesis Statement:**   **Grade:**   **4**   **Exceeds Standards**

This thesis statement directly and clearly responds to the prompt and provides reasons for the answer. The reader is interested to continue reading.

II.   **Evidence Used:**   **Grade:**   **4**   **Exceeds Standards**

The essayist presents a strong argument, backed by much evidence.

III.   **Evidence Explained: Grade:**   **4**   **Exceeds Standards**

After each piece of evidence, the author goes into detail explaining how the evidence supports the thesis statement.

IV.   **Conclusion:**   **Grade:**   **3**   **Meets Standards**

For an unknown reader, the writer brings in a new idea in the conclusion. The author writes that in central Europe, outside ideas were not accepted during medieval times. The author does not back up this idea with evidence.

V.   **Prewriting Activities: Grade:**   **4**   **Exceeds Standards**

The author conducted much research for this essay.

VI.   **The Unwritten Category:**   **Grade: Nothing subtracted**

Grade for "Medieval Japan"

Thesis:	4 x 5 = 20
Evidence Used:	4 x 5 = 20
Evidence Explained:	4 x 5 = 20
Conclusion:	3 x 5 = 15
Prewriting Activities	4 x 5 = 20
Sub Total:	95
Spelling and Grammatical Errors:	
Total Grade:	**A** **95**

Student Essay #2

Question: Under the Shoguns, was medieval Japan violent or peaceful, open or closed, culturally rich or poor?

"Medieval Japan"

For a long time, shoguns made Japan a violent, closed, and culturally rich society. Shoguns were mean people who liked to tell others what to do. Under the Shoguns, Japan was a tough place to live in.

Shogun society in medieval Japan was violent, closed, and culturally rich. First of all, shoguns were powerful military generals who ruled Japan like dictators. Shoguns controlled everything. The shoguns were very tough warriors, who fought and controlled the land like European knights. Secondly, medieval Japan was a closed society. French Catholic missionaries arrived in Japan and started baptizing people. After awhile, there were alot of Japanese Catholics. However, the Shoguns didn't like the Catholics and hurt all Christians. Medieval Japan was culturally rich. Have you ever seen a bonsai tree? It comes from Japan. Have you ever seen a Japanese garden with all those rocks raked nicely? In conclusion, medieval Japan was violent, closed, and culturally rich.

Medieval Japan was violent, closed, and culturally rich.

Grade Notes for Essay #1 "Medieval Japan"

I.   Thesis Statement: Grade: 2   Approaching Standards

The thesis statement is made weak by the use of the words "For a long time." The uncertainty of a statement such as this informs the reader that the writer does not know when shoguns ruled Japan.

II.   Evidence Used: Grade: 1   Below Standards

The essayist presents no pieces of supporting evidence. There are no dates, no names of people, no places.

III.   Evidence Explained: Grade: 2   Approaching Standards

Even though the evidence is weak, the author makes an attempt to analyze what little evidence is presented.

IV.   Conclusion: Grade: 2   Approaching Standards

The author believes in minimalism, and receives a low grade because of his belief.

V.   Prewriting Activities: Grade: 2   Approaching Standards

Little effort is displayed in the prewriting activities.

VI.   The Unwritten Category: Grade: -5

Poor choice of words informs the reader that the author either doesn't care about how the essay sounds or is unable to write well.

Grade for "Medieval Japan"

Thesis:	2 x 5 = 10
Evidence Used:	1 x 5 = 5
Evidence Explained:	2 x 5 = 10
Conclusion:	2 x 5 = 10
Prewriting Activities	2 x 5 = 10
Sub Total:	45
Spelling and Grammatical Errors:	-5
Total Grade:	**F 40**

The Five-Paragraph Essay

The five-paragraph is the standard for essay tests in secondary schools. Once a student can master this essay, all writing assignments will be made easier throughout the student's academic career, including at the university level. Below are two examples of five-paragraph essays based on a question from this book.

Grading Categories for a Five-Paragraph Essay

The grading categories for a five-paragraph essay differ from the one and three-paragraph essays primarily to make the grading easier for the teacher. The teacher grades each paragraph separately, grading as he reads. Saving valuable time, the teacher does not have to go back to different parts of the essay after he has read it. Please refer to the grading rubric in this book for more detail.

Paragraph I.   Thesis Statement and Interest

Is there a thesis statement and is the paragraph interesting?

Paragraph II.   Topic Sentence, Evidence, Closer

Does the paragraph contain a topic sentence, supporting evidence, explanations of the evidence, and a closer?

Paragraph III. Topic Sentence, Evidence, Closer

Does the paragraph contain a topic sentence, supporting evidence, explanations of the evidence, and a closer?

Paragraph IV. Topic Sentence, Evidence, Closer

Does the paragraph contain a topic sentence, supporting evidence, explanations of the evidence, and a closer?

Paragraph V   Restating Thesis Statement and Closer

Spelling or Grammatical Errors?

Do spelling or grammatical errors detract from the essay content?

Question: During the time of the Renaissance, what three aspects of life changed the most?

Student Essay #1

"Change in the Renaissance"

During the Renaissance in Europe, three aspects of life that changed the most were philosophy, the Christian Church, and discoveries and explorations of new lands. Roughly spanning the period 1300–1700, the Renaissance was a time of huge changes. Man's understanding of religion, philosophy, scientific knowledge, and the arts changed dramatically. The philosophy of humanism took a central role in man's endeavors and influenced all aspects of his life. This philosophy impacted his view of religion and of the world.

The greatest change during the Renaissance was in philosophy. Before the 1300s, Europeans placed their religious beliefs at the center of their lives. If the Catholic Church was against a particular way of learning or thinking, Europeans would follow. For instance, Pope Gregory VII forced King Henry IV in the eleventh century to beg for forgiveness, because the Pope had taken the king's power away by excommunicating him. During the Renaissance, however, humanism became the main philosophy of Europeans. Humanism placed the individual at the center of humanity, not Jesus Christ and the Church. Humanists glorified the individual and promoted self-improvement through learning. Some humanist writers were Francesco Petrarch and Giovanni Boccaccio. Humanists persuaded Europeans to explore their own mind and their world and not to rely solely on religion.

A second change during the Renaissance was the breakup of the Catholic Church. From the time of the collapse of the Roman Empire (A.D. 476) up until 1527, the Catholic Church had great power in Europe. A Catholic priest named Martin Luther spurred a radical change in religion and philosophy by breaking away from the Church and spurring religious wars. Luther protested against the Church for abuses involving misuse of money and power, and for not following the teachings of Jesus. Followers of Martin Luther became the architects of the Lutheran Church and leaders of the movement known as the Reformation. Those who protested and left the Catholic Church were known as "Protestants." Soon, other Protestant Churches formed, such as the Calvinist Church, the Anglican Church, and the Dutch Reformed Church. The breakup of the Catholic Church into many Christian Churches in Europe was a major change for Europeans.

    Thirdly, European explorers opened up the rest of the world by sailing around the globe and discovering and mapping lands. The countries of Portugal, Spain Holland, England and France competed for discovering and colonizing new lands. Portugal had a head start on the other countries in part due to Prince Henry the Navigator of the late 1400s. Portuguese Bartolomeu Dias sailed around the tip of Africa and opened up a sea route to India. Fernando Magellan led an expedition that circled the globe. Christopher Columbus sailed for the Spanish and discovered North and South America. These discoveries led to the colonization of many new lands, bringing power and wealth to Europe, and altering or ending life for the natives.

    In conclusion, the time of the Renaissance saw incredible changes. Changes in philosophy, religion, and knowledge of the physical world created a new world for mankind. Rapidly, reality for Europeans and for the rest of humanity altered. In Europe, no longer was religion at the center of all life. Humanists placed the individual in the most prominent position. No longer was there one Christian Church. The Catholic Church became one of many. And, exploration opened up the world for Europeans and changed the lives of those people who were colonized.

Grading Notes for Student Essay #1 "Change in the Renaissance"
Paragraph I.　　　**Thesis Statement and Interest**
Grade:　　4　　**Exceeds Standards**
The Thesis Statement answers the question clearly and provides evidence. It is interesting and hooks the reader into the essay.
Paragraph II.　　　**Topic Sentence, Evidence, Closer**
Grade: 3.5　　**Exceeds Standards**
The student uses a good amount of supporting evidence, explains it clearly, and has a strong closer. I am curious at the end of this paragraph what Francesco Petrarch and Giovanni Boccaccio wrote.
Paragraph III. Topic Sentence, Evidence, Closer
Grade: 4　　**Exceeds Standards**
The writer begins with a topic sentence, uses supporting evidence, explains this evidence very clearly, and finishes with a strong closer.
Paragraph IV. Topic Sentence, Evidence, Closer
Grade: 4　　**Exceeds Standards**
The essayist presents topic sentence, uses supporting evidence, explains this evidence very clearly, and finishes with a strong closer.
Paragraph V　　　**Restating Thesis Statement and Closer**
Grade: 4　　**Exceeds Standards**
This terrific conclusion is exemplary of a student who has good understanding of the topic.
Spelling or Grammatical Errors? No errors detract from the content.
Grade for "Change in the Renaissance"
Paragraph I.　　　　4　x　5 = 20
Paragraph II.　　　　4　x　5 = 20
Paragraph III.　　　　4　x　5 = 20
Paragraph IV.　　　　4　x　5 = 20

Paragraph V.   4   x   5 = 20
Total   A+   100

Student Essay #2

Question: During the time of the Renaissance, what three aspects of life changed the most?

"The Renaissance"

During the time of the Renaissance, three things changed the most. These changes happened in europe. They were big. One was the science, one was map making, and one was the printing press.

Science changed a lot in europe. Before the Renaissance, people used to listen to priests all the time. Whatever the priest said was like law. When Galileo said that the sun was the center, he got into trouble. The Catholics treated him real bad. But he said he didn't care what they thought about him, and he did it anyways. Because of Galileo, we could go to the moon.

Another thing that changed was making maps. Before Columbus, everybody thought the world was flat. Sailors were afraid to travel around globe. They talked about sea monsters swallowing up whole ships. They talked about ships falling off the end of the earth. When Columbus saw America, everything changed. They knew the world was round. People weren't afraid to sail anymore. And map making got a lot better.The printing press was a thing that made making books a lot easier. Before the printing press, not many people could read and write. After the printing press, many people could. When the printing press came around, life got better.

In conclusion, three things that changed the most during the Renaissance were science, map making, and the printing press. After the Renaissance, life was much easier.

Grading Notes for Student Essay #1 "Change in the Renaissance"

I.   Paragraph I: Grade: 2   Approaching Standards

The essayist takes a minimalist approach with this thesis statement. The brevity of this paragraph makes me question if the writer knows the topic well. Also, word choice is poor.

II.   Paragraph II: Grade: 1   Below Standards

The essayist presents an incredibly poor paragraph, with very poor word choices.

III.   Paragraph III: Grade: 1   Below Standards

It is difficult to grade the individual parts of this essay better than a one or a two. Again, evidence presented is weak, explanation is poor, and vocabulary is horrible.

IV.   Paragraph IV: Grade: 1   Below Standards

It appears this student did not try.

V.   Paragraph V: Grade: 2.5   Approaching Standards

At least this student chose three aspects of life in the Renaissance that changed.

VI.   Grammar/Spelling Errors   -5

Grade for "The Renaissance"

Paragraph I.   2   x   5 = 10
Paragraph II.   1   x   5 = 5
Paragraph III.   1   x   5 = 5
Paragraph IV.   1   x   5 = 5
Paragraph V.   2.5 x   5 =12.5
Subtotal   37.5
Grammar/Spelling Errors   -5
Total   F   32.5

Essays from American History from the Revolution up to 1914

Following are essays written by eighth-grade students.

Question: Was George Washington greatly responsible for the founding of the United States of America?

Student Essay #1

"George Washington – Not Responsible"

George Washington was not greatly responsible for the founding of the U.S. because he did not write the Declaration of Independence, France helped him at Yorktown, Thomas Paine wrote "Common Sense" which fired up the troops, he wasn't at the Boston Tea Party, and didn't start the Great Awakening. First of all, Thomas Jefferson wrote the declaration of independence. And, gave us our freedom that we have today. Secondly, the French advised him to attack Cornwallis at Yorktown. Other wise he would have lost in New York. Thirdly, Thomas Paine wrote "Common Sense" that fired up the troops. Which gave them the reason for fighting. In addition, George Washington was not present at the Boston tea party. Neither did he start the great awakening. So, as you see with out the Boston Tea party, the Declaration of Independence, "Common Sense" or the Boston massacre the U.S. wouldn't be were it is now.

Student Essay #2

"George Washington – Greatly Responsible"

George Washington was greatly responsible for the founding of the United States of America because of his loyalty, bravery, and cleverness. First of all, Washington bravely led the crossing of the Delaware River on Christmas night, December 25, 1776. This was important because George Washington captured the enemy at Trenton, New Jersey when it seemed like the Americans were losing the war. This event brought hope to Washington and his army. Secondly, Washington was a clever general and was nicknamed "the Silver Fox." During the first few years of the war, Washington's army was trapped in New York, and it appeared that the British would capture him and end the war. Washington kept fires burning at the American camp throughout the night, and in the meantime every soldier snuck away by boat. Furthermore, to end the war, Washington pretended to attack New York, but instead marched on the British at Yorktown while the French fleet cut off the British escape to the sea. In 1781, Washington scored the major victory of the war, capturing Cornwallis and a huge British army. Thirdly, Washington was loyal. Towards the end of the war, some in his army proposed for him to become a king. Washington refused this. As America's first president, Washington also refused to remain for a third term as President. He believed a republican government should not have one leader for too many years. In conclusion, Washington's actions during the American Revolution and his behavior during the first few years of the young republic were essential to the founding of the new republic, the United States of America.

Before looking at the next page, use the Grading Rubric to assess the two essays! Then, compare how you assessed the papers with how Mr. De Gree did. It is alright if you disagree with Mr. De Gree, as long as you don't fail a paper when he passed it.

John De Gree's Grading Notes for "George Washington – Not Responsible"

I. Thesis Statement: Grade: 3 Meets Standards

The thesis statement answers the question persuasively and provides pieces of supporting evidence. There are problems with grammar, however, and so this statement is not perfect.

II. Evidence Used: Grade: 3 Meets Standards

Are two or more relevant pieces of evidence used? The answer is yes. Although there are some problems with the evidence, the writer uses at least two pieces of evidence well. He writes that Thomas Jefferson wrote the Declaration of Independence. The author is inferring that more patriots besides George Washington were needed to make the American Revolution a success. The essayist also writes that Thomas Paine wrote "Common Sense." In this piece of evidence, the essayist is proving again that other Americans were necessary for the success of the American Revolution. There are problems with the remaining evidence used, so the grader should not count them positively towards the grade.

III. Evidence Explained: Grade: 2   Approaching Standards

Is the evidence explained correctly and persuasively? There are a number of problems in this category. The author states that it was Thomas Jefferson's Declaration of Independence gave us our freedoms today. This is somewhat of a stretch. The essayist offers us no proof that France told Washington to attack Cornwallis at Yorktown. Which general told Washington? At what meeting did it take place? The essayist states that Washington was not present at the Boston Tea Party, and that he did not start the Great Awakening. Yet, the author does not describe how these events led to the success of the American Revolution.

IV. Conclusion: Grade: 2.5   Approaching Standards

The conclusion doesn't sum up the main points of the essay entirely. The essayist should have written that other factors besides the life of George Washington led to the success of the American Revolution. The author also brings in a new piece of supporting evidence, the Boston Massacre. The conclusion should not bring in any new piece of evidence that was not explained in detail in the body of the essay. Also, it is difficult to understand the essayist due to spelling and grammatical errors.

V. Prewriting Activities: Grade   4   Exceeds Standards

This particular student completed all prewriting activities and researched in multiple sources.

VI. The Unwritten Category: -5

This student wrote with grammatical and spelling errors and sometimes sentences were awkward. Still, he was able to convey the content effectively.

Grade for "George Washington – Not Responsible"

Thesis:	3	x	5 =	15	
Evidence Used:		3	x	5 =	15
Evidence Explained:	2	x	5 =	10	
Conclusion:	2.5	x	5 =	12.5	
Prewriting Activities	4	x	5 =	20	
Sub Total:				72.5	
Spelling and Grammatical Errors:				-5	
Total Grade:	**C-**			**67.5**	

John De Gree's Grade for "George Washington – Greatly Responsible"

I. Thesis Statement: Grade: 4   Exceeds Standards

This student clearly answers the prompt and provides insight as to what the essay will be about.

II. Evidence Used: Grade: 4   Exceeds Standards

Convincing evidence is presented. Historical names, dates, and places are used to support the evidence.

III. Evidence Explained: Grade: 4   Exceeds Standards

This student shows that he grasps the content.

IV. Conclusion: Grade: 4   Exceeds Standards
The author shows that good writing can be interesting, even at the last sentence.
V. Prewriting Activities: Grade   4   Exceeds Standards
This particular student completed all prewriting activities.
VI. The Unwritten Category: Nothing detracted from the content.
Grade for "George Washington – Not Responsible"

Thesis:	4	x 5 =	20	
Evidence Used:	4	x 5 =	20	
Evidence Explained:	4	x 5 =	20	
Conclusion:	4	x 5 =	20	
Prewriting Activities	4	x 5 =	20	
Sub Total:			100	
Spelling and Grammatical Errors:				
Total Grade:	A+		**100**	

Five-Paragraph Essays From The American Revolution up to 1914

Question: What were the greatest three challenges to the young nation, 1789-1825?
Essay #1

"The Young Nation"

    The three greatest challenges that faced the young United States of America were the War of 1812, the Whisky Rebellion, and the Alien and Sedition Acts. These three challenges could have brought any new country complete ruin. The War of 1812 has been called "The Second American Revolution" because the British did not respect us, yet. The Whisky Rebellion could have started a Civil War. The Alien and Sedition Acts was a threat against the very principles that our country was founded on.

    The War of 1812 was a big challenge for the young nation to take on because the young nation had to at war with Great Britain shortly after the American Revolution. First of all, Henry Clay the war hawk felt that Great Britain was not treating the United States fairly and he thought that a war was the only thing that would earn us respect. Great Britain was treating the United Sates unfairly because great Britain was impressing American sailors and seizing our ships. Great Britain had the strongest navy in the world. America only had about 16 ships. Even though America was up against great odds, the American navy defeated the British navy. Captain Perry in the battle of Lake Erie defeated a British fleet and uttered the memorable words, "We have met the enemy and they are ours." On land, Andrew Jackson led American soldiers to defeat the British and their Indian allies. Jackson defeated the great Indian leader, Tecumseh. He also led the Americans to destroy the British at the Battle of New Orleans in 1815, killing over 2,000 British soldiers and only losing 7 Americans. The War of 1812 was a great challenge to the young nation that the United States of America succeeded in overcoming.

    A second big challenge that the young nation had to face was the Whisky Rebellion. This was a big challenge for the young nation because Americans wanted to fight each other. Congress passed a law placing a tax on whisky. Farmers and whisky makers did not like this law. Throughout Pittsburgh protesters gathered with guns, and threatened to destroy public buildings. George Washington reacted to this threat to the government by marching 15,000 American soldiers towards the rebels. Seeing what they were up against, the rebels disbanded. In this challenge, the supremacy of the federal government was threatened, but Washington solved the problem by a show of force. The second greatest challenge to the young republic was the Whisky Rebellion.

The third greatest challenge for the young nation was the Alien and Sedition Act. In 1798, the Federalists pushed this Act through Congress. This law allowed the president to kick out any immigrant or foreigner for any reason. It also allowed the president to jail anybody who spoke or wrote against the government. This was a horrible law that went directly against one of the main reasons for the American Revolution. One reason the founding fathers struggled for independence against Great Britain was so that each person would be free to express himself in words. The First Amendment guarantees Americans freedom of speech and press. This law took these freedoms away, and became a law that was actually unconstitutional. Also, it denied legal immigrants fair and just treatment. The Alien and Sedition Acts were a great challenge to our young nation. Fortunately, under Thomas Jefferson as President, this Act expired.

In conclusion, the three greatest challenges to the United States as a young nation were the War of 1812, the Whisky Rebellion, and the Alien and Sedition Acts. One challenge involved foreign affairs and two domestic. Also called the Second American Revolution, the War of 1812 could have meant dependence on Great Britain, or loss of territory, if America would have lost. The Whisky Rebellion was a great test of strength of the American government. And, the Alien and Sedition Act was a test of whether a country born with the ideas of freedom could withstand an overzealous government.

Essay #2

"The Young Nation"

The three greatest challenges to the young nation were the Alien and Sedition Act because the President was allowed to kick out an illegal immigrant, Jefferson because he was the first Secretary of State and the Whiskey Rebellion because Americans rebelled.

The greatest challenge was the Alien and Sedition Act because the President was allowed to kick out or expel any illegal immigrant. This is when the president can tell any illegal immigrant to go back home. President was also able to jail any person that wrote or speaked against the U.S. This meant that if any persono wrote something bad about the U.S. they would go to jail and also for speaking against. They would also say that immigrants were "Alien." They would say that because alien invade and immigrant come in from another country. John Adams was known for the Alien and Sedition. In 1801-1816 when Jefferson was president he let the Act expire. This Act was powerful towards illegal immigrants.

Jefferson was the second greatest challenge because he was the first Secretary of State. Jefferson then became president in 1801. He tried to appear more common. Jefferson passed the Embargo Act. In 1803 he bought Louisiana. He brought it so he could double the size of the U.S. This land was brought from Napoleon Bonaparte. In 1804 he sent Lewis and Clark to explore the Louisiana Territory. Sacagawea was the Indian guide that led them around territory. This opened the west up for settlement. Jefferson changed the U.S. during his Presidency in 1801-1816.

The third greatest challenge was the Whiskey rebellion because Americans rebelled. They did this because the whiskey was taxed. Americans didn't like that and were very angry. Washington heard that they were going to rebel so he marched with 15,000 and they rebelled. People didn't want to fight back because they were scared. This was a challenge because of Americans were rebelling.

The greatest challenge to the young nation was Alien and Sedition Act because any illegal immigrant can get kicked or expelled from the U.S., Jefferson because he was the first Secretary of State and Whiskey Rebellion because Americans rebelled. These were really tough challenges towards many Americans.

Using the Grading Scale, Grade the Two Essays above on your own. Then, check the following pages to see how John De Gree graded the papers.

John De Gree's Notes for Student Essay #1 "The Young Nation"
I. Paragraph I: Grade: 4   Exceeds Standards
The student does an excellent job answering the question and giving three reasons for the answer.
II. Paragraph II: Grade: 4   Exceeds Standards
A large amount of supporting evidence is used to support the topic sentence.
III. Paragraph III: Grade: 4   Exceeds Standards
The student uses great analytical skills, explaining the dangers of the whisky rebellion.
IV. Paragraph IV: Grade: 4   Exceeds Standards
The student crafts a strong argument, using evidence and explaining its importance.
V. Paragraph V: Grade: 4   Exceeds Standards
The student pulls off an outstanding paper with a terrific conclusion.
VI. Grammar/Spelling Errors   -3
When a paper is as good as this, the teacher can be stricter in this area. There are minor errors with grammar and punctuation, subject-verb agreement, and a missing word.

Grade for Student Essay #1

Paragraph I:	4	x	5= 20
Paragraph II:	4	x	5= 20
Paragraph III:	4	x	5= 20
Paragraph IV:	4	x	5= 20
Paragraph V:	4	x	5= 20
Subtotal:			100
Grammar/Spelling Errors			-3
Total Score:	A+		97

John De Gree's Notes for Student Essay #2 "The Young Nation"

I. Paragraph I: Grade: 2.5   Approaching Standards

This student's thesis statement is confusing. To make the claim that Jefferson was one of the top three challenges to the young nation because he was the first Secretary of State does not make sense. The student should spend more time here explaining what he means. Also, the thesis would have been more understandable to read if the writer had broken up the various ideas into multiple sentences.

II. Paragraph II: Grade: 2.5   Approaching Standards

This paragraph describes the Alien and Sedition Act as it relates to treatment of immigrants and of somebody speaking against the government, but there is no explanation of why these aspects are bad. The writer should have written something such as, "America should have been known as a place where immigrants were welcome because immigrants founded our country. It was wrong to take civil rights away from those not born on American soil." Also, the writer could have added, "To lock somebody up for speaking against the government is clearly a violation of the First Amendment guarantee of freedom of speech. It is wrong to not be able to say what you think." Without statements such as these, it is hard to see if the writer understands what he is writing.

III. Paragraph III: Grade: 1   Below Standards

Unfortunately, it appears that the student misunderstood the word challenge as it relates to Thomas Jefferson and the young republic.

IV. Paragraph IV: Grade: 3   Meets Standards

The topic sentence clearly states the third challenge and there is some explanation about what the rebellion was about. The writer could have done a better job at explaining how this rebellion was a threat to the new government, describing how many rebels there were, and telling in what state it happened.

V. Paragraph V: Grade: 2.5   Approaching Standards

This receives the same exact grade as Paragraph I because it is written with almost exactly the same words.

VI. Grammar/Spelling Errors   No errors detracted from content

Although there were errors in this essay, the errors didn't take away from the poor quality of the content.

XII. The Essential Tools of Literary Analysis

(Note: While teaching how to lead the Socratic discussion in history, I am usually asked to give my advice on how to teach the Socratic discussion in literature. Here are my recommendations.)

A. **Plot**

In nearly all short stories and novels your children and you will read, the story line follows a similar pattern. In the beginning of the story is Exposition. In exposition, the reader learns about the past of the characters and anything else that is important to the story. **Conflict** is also introduced. The conflict is the main problem of the story. There are many types of conflicts, such as man v. man, man v. nature, man v. society, man v. himself. Usually, in children's literature, it involves a young character trying to do something that is challenging for him to overcome. The solution to the conflict is called **Resolution**.

As the story progresses, certain events occur that keep the readers interest. These events usually happen to the main characters and are somewhat related to the conflict. These are called **Rising Action**.

The most exciting part of the story is called the **Climax**. In the story *Where the Red Fern Grows,* the climax can be the part during the competition where the Uncle is lost and the dogs have trapped three raccoons up in the tree. In *The Door in the Wall*, it is the battle. In the 1970s movie *Jaws*, it is the part where the main character fights the shark and kills it by blowing it up.

After the climax, the writer typically lets the reader know the outcome of the story. This is called **Falling Action**. In *Where the Red Fern Grows*, the two dogs pass away, the family is able to move out of the Ozarks, and we learn that a red fern grows in between the graves of the two dogs. In *The Door in the Wall*, we learn that the boy is honored by his parents and the entire kingdom, and the boy learns that his parents love and respect him, even though he cannot become a knight. In *Jaws*, we learn that the scientist along with the sheriff survive, and kick their way back home, out of the ocean.

Each story follows this basic pattern. See the Plot Chart on the next page. This chart allows the reader to see how an author uses this typical pattern to create a complete story.

Plot Chart

B. **Character**

How does an author let us know the personality of a character? A **character** speaks, thinks, acts, and feels. The author teaches us what type of person the character is through his words, his thoughts, his actions, and his feelings.

C. **Setting**

Setting refers to the time and place of a story. When does the story take place? What year is it? Which season does it take place in? What time of the day does it take place in? Where does it take place? Does it take place in a particular country, a particular part of the world? Is the setting important in the story or could it take place anywhere?

D. **Theme**

Theme refers to the message of the story. There can be many possible themes in a story. For this topic, it may be easiest to have a discussion. A possible theme to *Where the Red Fern Grows* is "Love between an animal and a human can teach us a lot about true love." Or the theme could be "A youth's pure heart can inspire adults to great love."

Analyzing a Short Story

To have a simple discussion without any written work on a short story or novel, start by asking your student to describe what the plot of the story was using the terms conflict, climax, rising action, falling action, and resolution. The student may write his answers right on the plot chart, if it is appropriate. Then, ask the student to describe the character and the setting. Ask the student to describe what a possible theme is. Ask for examples from the story that prove that the theme the student chose can be correct. If there is more time, the student can first fill out the following forms, and then report on them orally or he can report to the family at the dinner table.

Once a week, I drive my two daughters to their grandma's or aunt's house. During the 30 minute drive, if they have finished a book in the last week, we talk about what book they have read. My daughters tell me about the plot, a character the setting, and the theme. I ask them to give me examples from the book so that I can see the plot, or character, or setting, or theme, better. If I have more time, I ask my daughters interpretive questions about the story, and I compel them to defend their answer by pointing out where they got their answer from the text. Questions with an asterisk preceding them can be used for family discussions at the dinner table. For all answers, be prepared to show where in the story you found your answer. You may cite the paragraph. For each answer, please be ready to explain why you think this is the answer.

Plot

1. What is the plot of the story? To answer this, answer the following questions:
    a. What is the conflict?
    b. What is one rising action?
    c. What is the climax?

    d. What is one falling action?
    e. What is the resolution?

Character

1. Choose a character from this story.
2. What does he or she look like?
3. What is his personality?
4. What is something the character in the story says that tells you what his personality is like?
5. Are there any other characters in the story that like or dislike this character? Explain.
6. Do you like or dislike this character? Why?
7. If it were possible to know this character personally, do you think you would be his friend? Why or why not?
8. What are some characteristics about this character that you admire and would like to emulate?
9. What are some characteristics about this character that you don't admire and would not like to emulate?
*10. Describe this character to your family at the dinner table or at the next possible opportunity. Ask somebody in your family if he thinks this character would make a good friend for you. Have the person in your family explain their answer. After he explains his answer, let him know if you agree or disagree with him. Ask if this character reminds him of somebody he knows. Ask him to explain why.

Setting

1. When does the story take place?
2. What year is it?
3. Which season does it take place in?
4. What time of the day does it take place in?
5. Where does it take place?
6. Does it take place in a particular country, a particular part of the world?
7. Is the setting important in the story or could it take place anywhere?

Theme

1. What is a possible theme of this story?
2. Describe an event or events in this story that led you to think of a theme to this story.
3. Can you apply this theme in your life? How might it apply today in your life?
4. Do you think this theme is one that could benefit your family members if they know it? How?
*5. Share with your family the theme of this story and share how you might use this message in your life. Ask somebody in your family how they could apply it in their lives today during dinner.

XIII. Encouraging Family Discussion at the Dinner Table

There are many important reasons for the family to discuss academic subjects with each other. Parents learn what their children think and the process in which the children are making decisions. The subject is not personal so it allows the student to speak without being embarrassed by revealing anything personal they might not want to. In addition, children learn the thought processes of their parents, and parents are able to impart on their children lessons about life they might not ever get the chance to.

In my 20 years of teaching youth, one constant has remained. Those kids who have dinner with their entire family tend to do better in school, are more patient with others, have better thinking processes than other students, and tend to make better social choices.

Because Mom or Dad may be exhausted by dinner time, family discussion could be started by a child. When a child finishes reading a book, he can present his answers to the theme questions to the family. Question #5 is:

> Share with your family the theme of this story and ask them how they could apply it in their lives. Ask anyone you want to at the dinner table, or the next time you are all together. This may start a conversation about how we should treat others.

Likewise, Question # 11 from Character is:

> Describe this character to your family at the dinner table or at the next possible opportunity. Ask somebody in your family if he thinks this character would make a good friend for you. Have the person in your family explain their answer. After he explains his answer, let him know if you agree or disagree with him.

When a student finishes an assignment involving the classical education in history, he needs to present it to the entire family, along with his findings. Each person around the table should be compelled to ask some type of question to the presenter. This may start a discussion as it is possible one of the parents has an opinion on this topic that goes against or confirms the child's paper.

Or, for a discussion in current events, the parent or child can choose something that is happening and ask a question involving the idea "Cause and Effect." For example, "What is causing gas prices to rise?" Or, "Why is there unrest in the Middle East?" It may be that nobody will know the answer. If this is the case, a parent can assign this as an "extra credit" question for the kids and parents to research for the next day's dinner table topic.

Let's imagine right now a variety of "Cause and Effect" questions we could generate involving current events and share them with each other.

Made in the USA
San Bernardino, CA
28 July 2020